Fuck
A History of Swearing

Dr. Alex Aaronson

Panjandrum
Publishing

Contents

Forward: The Power of Words

Ah, words! Those little buggers that march out of our mouths with all the pomp and circumstance of a parade; sometimes, they're like fireworks in the night sky, illuminating the darkest corners of our souls. And sometimes, those words are like arrows, aimed at the heart of convention and decorum, fired by the rebels, the troublemakers, and the jesters of society. This is a book about those words – the ones that dance on the edge of respectability and linger in the deepest recesses of our language, those little darlings that society tells us we mustn't say but secretly can't resist.

You might be wondering why a book on the history and significance of swear words needs to exist. After all, in a world bursting with encyclopedias, almanacs, and guides to everything under the sun, do we really need a manual on profanity? The answer, dear reader, is a resounding 'Fuck yeah!'

Why, you ask? Because swearing is a lens through which we can peer into the inner workings of society, an x-ray of our collective psyche. Swearing is, in essence, a vibrant and living form of folk culture. It's the unvarnished, unfiltered expression of human emotion, a raw reaction to life's absurdities and frustrations. Swearing, you see, isn't just about using certain words; it's about rebellion, release, and reclamation. It is the vocabulary of the Id and the Shadow.

As we embark on this journey through the annals of obscenity, let us remember that swearing has been with us for as long as language itself. The history of swearing is as old as humanity, perhaps older if you can imagine what Homo Erectus ejaculated when he burnt himself on the first fire or cut his finger on a finely worked flint. It is a fertile landscape sculpted by rivers of anger, high mountains of joy, deep ravines of pain, and sunny horizons of pleasure. Just as humans have evolved over millennia, so too have our expletives and oaths.

In the beginning, there were primal grunts and gestures, the first inklings of communication. But as our ancestors' thoughts and emotions grew more complex, or may we say modern, so did their vocabulary. Early on, obscenities were likely simple noises reflecting the earthy, visceral nature of early existence. 'Shit' still elicits a snigger both verbally and actually in all ages and defanged 'poop' still raises a smile.

As civilizations bloomed and societies formed, so too did the pantheon of profanity expand. Swearing became a tool of rebellion against authority, a way for the powerless to lash out at the powerful. It was the commoner's cudgel against the aristocracy's rapier, the jester's jest, and the poet's flourish. Shakespeare himself was no stranger to a well-placed curse, adorning his plays with language aimed at riveting the attention of robust theatre goers inhabiting a theatre more like a sporting event than a gentile evening of refined culture.

But what, you might ask, is the current state of swearing? In our age of unprecedented connectivity and communication, profanity has taken on new dimensions. The internet, with its endless forums, social media platforms, and comment sections, has become a digital playground for linguistic transgressors. In this vast digital landscape, the boundaries of what's considered 'acceptable' language have stretched and blurred.

We live in a paradoxical era where both the proliferation of profanity and the narrow policing of language coexist. Social norms dictate that we must be careful with our words, and yet, there is a rebellious spirit, a yearning for authenticity, a frothing up of ill-considered interaction that leads us to unleash our inner verbal demons, often loaded with the most acid of bile.

Now, more than ever, we find ourselves at a crossroads, where swearing is both celebrated and condemned, where its usage can spark outrage or unite communities or pass unnoticed amongst the howl of random noise swirling around us. The lines between humor, offense and expression are more blurred than ever before.

So, why does swearing matter? It matters because it's a testament to our humanity and a large part of its basic vocabulary; a powerful form of punctuation not included in any book of grammar. It's the language of 'the people,' the unfiltered 'voice of the masses,' the unapologetic howl of emotion in a world where pressure to conformity creates backlash. Swearing reminds us that beneath our polished façades, we are raw, messy and imperfect creatures.

In a world that often feels fake and scripted, profanity serves as a reminder of the vitality and unpredictability of human language. It's a release valve for our frustrations, a burst of joy, a battle cry, and sometimes, just a good laugh. Swearing, in all its profane glory, is a testament to the enduring human spirit – the unquenchable flame of rebellion that refuses to be extinguished.

As we delve into the pages of this book, remember that swearing is not just about the words themselves; it's about the emotions, the stories, and the cultural contexts that give them power. It's about the rebels and the jesters who have used profanity to challenge authority and provoke thought.

So, dear reader, prepare to journey through time and language, as we explore the history, evolution, and significance of swearing. Let us embark on this linguistic adventure with an open mind and a sense of humor, for in the world of profanity, there's much to learn, much to unlearn and much to laugh about. After all, as the saying goes, 'Laughter is the best swear word.'

Introduction: What is Profanity?

Across the vibrant landscape of language, swear words stand as enigmatic and boisterous characters, participating in a linguistic dance that traverses eras and cultures. These lexical renegades, akin to masked revelers at a carnival, have undergone a transformation as vivid as it is mystifying – a masquerade that we shall now explore, accompanied by the echoes of etymology and linguistic evolution.

The Origin of 'Profanity': A Linguistic Odyssey

Our journey commences with the word 'profane,' an invitation to embark on a whimsical linguistic odyssey. Its roots stretch back to classical Latin, an archaic and enchanting tongue where 'profanus' takes center stage – a term adorned with dual connotations. 'Pro' beckons us 'outside,' while 'fanum' extends the invitation to leave the temple or sanctuary, prompting us to ponder being 'outside the temple.'

But what does it truly mean to be 'profane' in this bygone context? The answer, dear readers, is as beguiling as the Latin itself. 'Profanity' in its nascent form held two distinct meanings – it could signify 'desecrating what is holy' or 'pursuing secular purposes.' This linguistic chameleon made its grand entrance as early as the 1450s, a time when words held the power to sculpt perceptions and shape the very fabric of reality and literacy was practically non-existent.

From Sacred to Sinful: The Subtle Shift in Semantics

To embark on the journey of swear words, we must first distinguish between 'profanity' and its bolder sibling, 'blasphemy.' In bygone days, 'profanity' symbolized secular indifference towards religion or religious figures – an almost nonchalant linguistic shrug. In stark contrast, 'blasphemy' was the audacious assault on religion and its venerated figures – an act considered sinful, a direct contravention of the sacred Ten Commandments in the predominantly Christian

Western world. It could get you killed and certainly imprisoned. In parts of the world, it still can.

Within these ancient pages, we encounter a collection of Bible verses sternly admonishing the act of swearing. This disapproval emanated from the very heart of religious doctrine and moral teachings. To utter profanities or blasphemies was to invite the ire of the divine, a perilous endeavor in a world where faith reigned supreme and for the faithful, where the deity themselves could strike you down at a moment's notice.

Pagan Origins:
From Deities to Profanity

Yet, as the river of history winds through the epochs, we stumble upon a captivating metamorphosis in select corners of the globe. Profanity, it seems, often boasts pagan roots, which, under the imposing shadow of Christian influence, underwent a transformation. Words once reverentially whispered as the names of deities and spirits found themselves thrust into the profane limelight, adorned with masks of vulgarity and scorn.

Consider the illustrious Finnish profanity word 'perkele.' In ages past, it was believed to be the sacred name of Ukko, the thunder god and the chief deity of the Finnish pagan pantheon. In the intricate alchemy of linguistic evolution, this once-hallowed name donned the cloak of profanity – a transformation akin to a deity descending from the heavens to partake in earthly revelry.

A Tradition of Divine Mockery

To grasp the evolution of profanity fully, we must shift our gaze toward the ancient tradition of the comic cults. These joyous gatherings reveled in laughter, mirth and, above all, in scoffing at the divine – an irreverent celebration where deities themselves became the subjects of jest and satire. An exemplary instance of this theatrical revelry can be found in the works of Lucian, whose 'Dialogues of the Gods' stand as a testament to the power of laughter in the presence of the divine.

It can be seen in the rituals of the Roman Saturnalia, such as:

Role Reversal: One of the central features of the Saturnalia was the temporary overturning of social hierarchies. During the festival, slaves and masters would exchange roles, and servants were allowed to speak freely and even jest at their masters without fear of punishment. This role reversal created humorous and absurd situations that contributed to the festive spirit.

Feasting and Merrymaking: The Saturnalia was a time of feasting and indulgence. People would gather for lavish banquets, and excessive eating and drinking were common. Merrymaking, including singing, dancing and playing games, added to the joyful atmosphere.

Gift-Giving: Gift-giving was an integral part of the Saturnalia, and people exchanged small presents, known as 'sigillaria,' often in a playful and lighthearted manner. These gifts were typically inexpensive and sometimes humorous.

Joviality and Laughter: Laughter and mirth were encouraged during the Saturnalia. People engaged in jesting, storytelling and humorous performances. There were even contests for the wittiest jesters.

Satirical Plays: Some sources suggest that during the Saturnalia, comedic and satirical plays were performed. These plays might have mocked societal norms, political figures or cultural trends, adding an element of satire and humor to the festivities.

Further back in time we have the Greek Dionysian Festivals, which flourished during the 5th century BCE and beyond. These were vibrant celebrations dedicated to the god Dionysus, the Greek deity associated with wine, theater and revelry. These festivals were characterized by a unique blend of religious devotion, artistic expression and social commentary, making them a fascinating cultural phenomenon in ancient Greece.

The origins of the Dionysian festivals are rooted in ancient Greek mythology. Dionysus, also known as Bacchus in Roman mythology, was the god of wine, fertility and dramatic performance. His cult and festivals held a special place in Greek religious life. Dionysian rituals often involved the consumption of wine and the ecstatic celebration of the god's divine presence, the sort of behavior later considered profane by Christians which still today raises an eyebrow.

Satirical Comedies

One of the remarkable features of the Dionysian festivals was the performance of comedies, and no discussion of Greek comedy would be complete without mentioning Aristophanes. Aristophanes, a renowned playwright, used this platform to create satirical comedies that often targeted political figures, social issues, and cultural norms.

Aristophanes' comedies were known for their biting wit and sharp criticism of contemporary society. Through humor, wordplay and clever scenarios, he tackled issues such as the Peloponnesian War, the role of women in society, and the follies of political leaders. His works, including 'Lysistrata' and 'The Clouds,' provided a humorous lens through which the audience could examine and reflect on pressing issues of the time.

Within these dialogues, gods and goddesses discarded their divine robes to step into the arena of the absurd, their pompousness punctured by the keen blade of satire. It's a world where the divine is rendered delightfully human, and the sanctity of language is gleefully cast aside.

The Perpetual Masquerade of Words

As we bid adieu to this chapter, we stand at the precipice of linguistic history. Profanity, with its shifting meanings and audacious transformations, showcases the boundless elasticity of language. Words, akin to actors in an eternal masquerade, don masks of reverence, irreverence, and everything in between.

The Roots of Swear Words: A Linguistic Expedition

To unravel the intricate skein of swear words, we embark on a linguistic odyssey that spans across time and space. These seemingly irreverent and crude words have origins that are as diverse as they are captivating – a blend of history, culture and etymology that unveils the very essence of human expression.

In the vast realm of the English language, swear words like 'shit' boldly flaunt their Germanic roots, a heritage that stretches back through the annals of time. As for the infamous 'fuck,' it too is believed to have its origins nestled within the folds of Germanic languages, a linguistic enigma that has perplexed and fascinated scholars for centuries.

However, it is essential to acknowledge that the etymology of English profanity is a complex weave, incorporating threads from various linguistic lineages. Words such as 'damn' and 'piss,' for instance, take a more scenic route, journeying through Old French before finding their way into the English lexicon, ultimately owing their origins to the Latin tongue.

In the realm of technical and polite alternatives, Latin takes center stage. Words like 'defecate' or 'excrete' elegantly veil the act of expelling bodily waste (commonly referred to as 'shit') with a veneer of sophistication. Similarly, 'fornicate' and 'copulate' delicately allude to the intimate act that 'fuck' so brashly represents.

The Label of 'Anglo-Saxon': A Linguistic Stereotype

While it is true that many English swear words proudly bear Germanic roots, it is a sweeping generalization to apply this label to the entirety of English profanity. This dynamic language, ever-evolving and multifaceted, offers exceptions that defy categorization.

Enter the charming term 'wanker,' a colloquial gem in the British lexicon. Although it might be considered profane in contemporary Britain, its roots do not stretch back to the distant annals of linguistic history. No, dear readers, 'wanker' made its debut on the linguistic stage a mere blink of an eye ago, in the mid-20th century. This linguistic upstart challenges the notion that all English profanity harks back to ancient origins, highlighting the ever-evolving nature of language and the perpetual invention of new ways to express scorn and disdain.

The roots of swear words meander through time and culture, reflecting the intricacy of human expression. From the Germanic echoes of 'shit' and 'fuck' to the winding pathways of 'damn' and 'piss,' and the whimsical emergence of 'wanker,' each word carries with it a unique history, a cultural fingerprint, and a testament to the ever-shifting landscape of profanity.

Chapter 1:
Origins of Obscenity

In the beginning, there were words. Simple, primal grunts and gestures served as the earliest forms of communication. These rudimentary exchanges were the foundation upon which language was built, the humble beginnings of the intricate evolution of vocabulary that would evolve over millennia. But as our ancestors' thoughts and emotions grew more complex, so did their language, and inevitably, so did their curses.

The history of swearing is a journey through the labyrinthine corridors of human expression, a tale of words that strayed from the path of respectability and decorum, and a chronicle of the irrepressible spirit of rebellion that has been part and parcel of the human experience. To truly understand the nature of obscenity, we must journey back in time, to the very dawn of language itself.

The Dawn of Language

Picture, if you will, our ancient ancestors huddled around a campfire. The night is dark, the world mysterious, and danger lurks in the shadows. In such a harsh and unforgiving environment, communication was a matter of life and death. The earliest hominids would have communicated primarily through simple, guttural sounds and gestures – efficacious tools for signaling danger or expressing basic needs.

As our species evolved, so too did our communication. Our ancestors began to develop more complex forms of language, allowing them to convey not just immediate threats or desires but also abstract concepts and emotions. Words became a tool for understanding the world around them and expressing their innermost thoughts.

Yet, as with any great leap forward, the birth of language also brought forth a shadow – the emergence of obscenity. As humans developed the ability to express themselves more freely, they also discovered the liberating power of words that were not bound by convention or decorum. These early obscenities were no doubt simple, rooted in the raw, visceral experiences.

Primitive Profanities

Early obscenities, like modern ones, were often tied to bodily functions and sensations, the most elemental aspects of human existence. The use of such words, as today, served various purposes in primitive human society.

Firstly, they were a means of venting frustration and anger. Imagine an early human, struggling to start a fire in the pouring rain or being chased by a saber-toothed tiger. In such dire situations, an expletive or two would undoubtedly provide catharsis and, perhaps, a momentary psychological advantage.

Secondly, obscenities were used to describe the intense, sometimes painful, experiences of life. A sharp stone cutting the foot, a thorn piercing the hand or a stone-age gadget not cooperating as intended – all of these warranted a stream of colorful language. Such words were vivid and immediately expressed the emotion of physical suffering.

In addition to these practical applications, early obscenities also held a social function. They were a way for people to identify with their peers, to differentiate themselves from outsiders. Sharing a common obscenity would have been a bonding experience – it signified membership in a particular group or tribe, a shared understanding of the world's hardships, and a common language of frustration.

The Evolution of Swearing

As human societies became more organized and structured, so too did their languages. The roots of obscenity grew deeper. Different societies developed their own unique profanities, reflecting their values, taboos and fears.

In ancient Rome, for example, profanity often revolved around deities and the act of copulation. The Romans had a rich lexicon of obscenities and colorful phrases that celebrated the act of sex and its associated deities. They saw nothing sinful or shameful about discussing such matters openly.

Here are some they prepared earlier:

Futuere – To have sexual intercourse.

Cunnus – A vulgar term for female genitalia.

Penis – A reference to the male genitalia.

Irrumare – A graphic term for performing oral sex on a male.

Pedicare – To engage in anal intercourse.

Fellare – To perform oral sex on a male.

Mentula – A slang term for the male genitalia.

Labia – Referring to the female genital lips.
Podex – A colloquial word for the buttocks.
Testiculi – Testicles.
Cacare – To defecate or excrete.
Stercus – Feces or dung.
Merda – A vulgar term for excrement.
Micturire – To urinate.
Semen – Semen, the male reproductive fluid.
Cunnilingus – The act of performing oral sex on a female.
Fellatio – The act of performing oral sex on a male.
Coitus – Sexual intercourse.
Thrustus – A euphemism for the act of thrusting during sex.
Vulva – The female external genitalia.

In the Middle Ages, obscenities began to take on a more Christian flavor, with curses invoking the devil and his minions. Swearing on the Bible or making blasphemous statements became more taboo as the power of the Church grew.

Here be dragons:

Fīlþrag – A term for a foul or wicked person.
Hellebend – A reference to someone who belongs to Hell.
Fandian – To try or tempt someone, often in a sinful way.

Mōndǣdlīc – Meaning 'devilish' or 'demonic.'

Galdorcwide – A curse or spell, often invoking evil forces.
Wyrm – A serpent or dragon, sometimes symbolizing the devil.
Gāst – A spirit or ghost, often used negatively.
Sāwolcwēnan – To lament or cry out in anguish.

Hǣðen – A term for a non-Christian or heathen.

Hellegrind – The gates of Hell.
Grim – Meaning fierce or cruel.
Scīte – A term for excrement.
Hwætēow – Impure or vile.
Leahtrēow – A tree of evil or wickedness.
Sārcwide – A blasphemous or sacrilegious statement.
Fyren – Fiery or hellish.
Dēofolgyld – Devil-worship or idolatry.

Hǣþenscipe – Heathenism or non-Christian beliefs.

Gāstlīc – Ghostly or spectral.
Wite – Punishment or divine retribution.

During the Renaissance, the profane and the sacred danced an intricate minuet. Shakespeare himself was no stranger to a well-placed curse or two. His works are peppered with language reflecting the changing social norms and the emergence of new words and phrases that straddled the line between vulgarity and wit.

Here are some bard mouth phrases:

'Why, then the world's mine oyster, Which I with sword will open.' – *The Merry Wives of Windsor*. A metaphorical reference to sex.

'Thou art as fat as butter.' – *Henry IV*, Part 1. An insult, still likely to sting.

'The rankest compound of villainous smell that ever offended nostril.' – *The Merry Wives of Windsor*. Fart wouldn't have rhymed either.

'He is deformed, crooked, old, and sere, Ill-faced, worse bodied, shapeless everywhere.' – *Henry VI, Part 3*. An insult, the sort of thing that passes for swearing in many countries.

'She is spherical, like a globe. I could find out countries in her.' – *The Comedy of Errors*.

'Marry, sir, 'tis an ill cook that cannot lick his own fingers.' – *Romeo and Juliet*.

'Away, you three-inch fool!' – *The Taming of the Shrew*.

'You scullion! You rampallian! You fustilarian!' – *Henry IV, Part 2*. How rude these words were is now hard to benchmark, though the tone suggests they were meant to bite hard.

'Thou whoreson zed, thou unnecessary letter!' – *King Lear*.

'Thou art a base, proud, shallow, beggarly, three-suited, hundred-pound, filthy worsted-stocking knave; a lily-livered, action-taking knave; a whoreson, glass-gazing, super-serviceable finical rogue.' – *King Lear*. Unlike the Anglo-Saxon, the Latin, Middle Eastern, Japanese and even Russians are know for their 'creative swearing' through extended description, something that seems unnecessarily elaborate to the user of the two or three word epithet.

'Thou elvish-mark'd, abortive, rooting hog!' – *Richard III*. After 600 years Elvish is now a complement but then Shakespeare did not have the word 'Orc' to conjure with.

Famous Swearers in History

Throughout recorded history, there have been notable figures who were unabashed in their use of obscenities. These individuals often used their words to challenge the status quo or to emphasize a point. Here are a few examples:

Emperor Caligula: Caligula, known for his eccentric behavior and cruelty, was said to have used vulgar language and profanity regularly. His reign was marked by extravagance and excess, and he was not known for his restraint in his speech.

Emperor Nero: Nero, who ruled during a tumultuous period in Roman history, was known for his excesses and indulgences. While there may not be direct records of his swearing, his behavior and actions were often seen as scandalous and offensive.

Óðinn's Curse: In the saga of Egill Skallagrímsson, the protagonist, Egill, composes a poem in which he curses the Norwegian king, Eiríkr Bloodaxe. This poem is known as 'Egill's Curse' and includes strong language and curses directed at the king and his family.

Henry II of England (1133-1189): Henry II was known for his fiery temper and strong language. He famously had a contentious relationship with Thomas Becket, the Archbishop of Canterbury, and is said to have uttered the infamous words, 'Will no one rid me of this turbulent priest?' This statement was interpreted by some as an order to eliminate Becket, which led to his assassination.

Richard the Lionheart (1157-1199): Richard I, known as the Lionheart, was a skilled military leader but also had a reputation for using strong language and profanity. He engaged in various conflicts during his reign, including the Third Crusade.

Mark Twain: The famed American author was known for his irreverent humor and use of colorful language. In *The Adventures of Huckleberry Finn*, he wrote, 'All right, then, I'll go to hell,' a line that resonated with its defiance and bluntness.

Winston Churchill: The British Prime Minister was famous for his sharp wit and his penchant for peppering his speeches with profanity. His words provided solace and strength to a nation facing the dark days of World War II.

Lenny Bruce: Perhaps the first person to be made famous by swearing, an American stand-up comedian and social critic was known for pushing boundaries with his explicit and profanity-laden comedy routines, which often led to legal troubles.

George Carlin: This legendary stand-up comedian pushed the boundaries of language and societal norms in his routines. His 'Seven Dirty Words' sketch became an iconic commentary on censorship and freedom of speech.

Why Swearing Mattered Then

In the times of our ancestors, swearing mattered for several reasons. Firstly, it was a means of coping with the harsh realities of life. The visceral and immediate nature of obscenities allowed people to vent their frustrations, to release pent-up emotions and to maintain a semblance of control in the face of adversity.

Secondly, swearing served as a social bond. It was a way for people to connect, to express solidarity and to reinforce their shared experiences. It was a common language of suffering and celebration, a unifying force in a world fraught with dangers.

Swearing also played a role in challenging authority. In societies where certain words or ideas were considered taboo or blasphemous, the act of using profanity was a form of rebellion. It was a way to assert one's autonomy and to challenge the established norms of society, often with a healthy dose of humor and irreverence.

Why Swearing Matters Now

In our modern age, swearing continues to hold a unique and significant place in our language and culture. It matters now for reasons that echo the past and reflect our current societal dynamics.

Firstly, swearing remains a means of emotional release. In a world that can be overwhelming and frustrating, the act of uttering a well-placed expletive can provide a momentary catharsis, a release of pent-up tension, and a feeling of control in chaotic situations.

Secondly, swearing still serves as a social bond. It's a way for people to connect and identify with one another, to share a common language of humor and frustration. Whether it's among friends, coworkers or fellow enthusiasts, profanity can be a unifying force, a way to break down barriers and build camaraderie.

In addition, swearing continues to challenge authority and societal norms. It's a means of rebellion and defiance, a way to assert one's autonomy and question established conventions. Swearing can be a powerful tool for pushing the boundaries of language and freedom of expression.

Lastly, swearing has found new life in the realm of humor and entertainment. Comedians like George Carlin and Lenny Bruce, as well as contemporary stand-up artists, use profanity as a means of highlighting absurdities, critiquing society and eliciting laughter. Swearing has become an integral part of our comedic language, a way to punctuate jokes and provoke audience responses.

Conclusion: A Linguistic Rebellion

The history of swearing is a rich one. From our primitive ancestors' grunts and gestures to Shakespeare's eloquent curses, from the defiance of Winston Churchill to the irreverence of George Carlin, obscenities have played a unique and enduring role in our language and culture.

As we embark on this journey through the annals of profanity, remember that swearing is not just about the words themselves; it's about the emotions, the stories and the cultural contexts that give them power. It's a testament to the enduring human spirit – the unquenchable flame of rebellion that refuses to be extinguished.

Let us explore the origins of obscenity, the evolution of swearing and its continued importance in our modern world. Let us navigate the labyrinthine corridors of language and embrace the power of words that have been both whispered in shame and shouted in defiance. As we delve deeper into the pages of this book, may we do so with open minds, hearty laughter and a dash of irreverence, for in the world of profanity, there's much to learn, much to unlearn and much to laugh about.

Chapter 2:
Early Language Taboos

In vocabulary there exists a curious and colorful subset – taboo language. These are the words and phrases that society, in its wisdom (or lack thereof), has deemed unsuitable for polite company. Such words, though oftentimes simple and visceral, carry with them the weight of centuries of societal judgments and conventions.

As we delve into the second chapter of our linguistic journey, it's crucial to understand that what constitutes a 'swear word' or an obscenity is a matter as dynamic as the ever-shifting sands of language and culture itself. What shocks and appalls in one era may be innocuous or even quaint in another. So, dear reader, let us embark on a quest to explore the early taboos of language, the first recorded instances of swear words and the curious ways in which societies across the ages have grappled with them.

The Dawn of Swear Words

To truly grasp the nature of early taboos, we must first transport ourselves to a time when society was a primordial soup of cultures and languages. The first recorded instances of swear words are as diverse and complex as the civilizations that birthed them. These taboos often centered around the primal and the profane – life, death, sex and the human body.

Sumerian texts: These are some of the earliest written records in human history, yet do not contain swearing or profanity as we understand it in contemporary terms. But history would soon be in the making.

Assyrian Curse Tablets: Some ancient Assyrian curse tablets have been discovered, which contain curses and imprecations aimed at individuals believed to have wronged the person creating the tablet. These curses often invoke the gods to bring harm or misfortune to the targeted individuals.

Ancient Egypt: In the fertile lands along the Nile, the ancient Egyptians had their share of forbidden utterances. One such taboo word revolved around the excrement of animals. Mentioning these foul substances was considered disrespectful and impolite, as it could potentially offend the sacred animals, which were highly revered.

Ancient Greece: The Greeks, known for their rich literary tradition and philosophical musings, had their own set of language taboos. Obscene words often referred to bodily functions and sexual acts. Euphemisms were commonly employed to discuss such matters in a more polite and indirect manner. Even in the bawdy comedies of Aristophanes, the use of obscenities was carefully orchestrated for comedic effect.

Ancient China: The Chinese civilization, with its ancient wisdom and complex system of hieroglyphic characters, also had its share of linguistic taboos. Swearing or using vulgar language was considered a sign of low breeding and a lack of moral character. It was particularly frowned upon in the context of formal communication and literature.

The Romans: In the heart of the Roman Empire, where Latin was the lingua franca, obscenities were aplenty. The Latin language was rife with words related to bodily functions and sexual acts. Still, there were varying degrees of acceptability, and the choice of words could denote one's social class and education level.

Early Taboos and Their Significance

The early taboos surrounding language were not arbitrary. They were deeply rooted in cultural, religious, and social values. Let's explore why these particular words and phrases were deemed obscene by the people of their respective times.

Religious Significance: In many societies, words associated with deities, sacred rituals and the divine were considered off-limits. Uttering them inappropriately was seen as blasphemous and sacrilegious. This concept extended to anything that tainted the purity of religious language.

Social Hierarchy: Swearing often became a tool for differentiating between social classes. The nobility and educated elite were expected to use refined and cultured language, while the common folk might use cruder expressions. Swearing, in this context, reinforced societal hierarchies.

Hygiene and Health: Words related to bodily excretions and functions were frequently taboo due to concerns about cleanliness and health. Early societies had limited knowledge of sanitation, and contact with human waste was a significant health risk. Thus, such words carried with them the taboo of the unclean.

Cultural Norms: Language taboos also reflected cultural norms and values. For instance, in some cultures, openly discussing sexual matters was seen as immodest and inappropriate. In others, it was considered a natural and healthy part of communication. Likewise, anatomical terms are considered OK, while their non-scientific counterparts are considered obscene.

Power and Control: The use of profanity was sometimes employed as a means of asserting dominance or challenging authority. Swearing could be a form of rebellion against the status quo, a means of expressing frustration with those in power or as a way of reenforcing dominance through verbal violence.

The Evolution of Taboos

As societies evolved and languages developed, so too did the taboos surrounding language. Swearing and obscenity continued to play a pivotal role in the dynamics of power, class, and culture. In medieval Europe, for example, the Catholic Church held tremendous influence, and blasphemy was considered a grave sin. The act of taking the Lord's name in vain or using obscene language was not only offensive but also heretical, which in turn was dangerous for all parties, not just in this life but also in the one projected to occur after death.

During the Renaissance, the lines between the sacred and the profane began to blur. The newfound fascination with the classical world and humanism led to a resurgence of interest in ancient Greek and Roman literature, some of which contained explicit language and themes. This period of cultural reawakening brought with it a more open discussion of taboo subjects in literature and the arts.

Throughout history, famous figures have not been immune to the allure of swearing and the breaking of taboos. Here are a few examples:

Chaucer's 'The Canterbury Tales': Geoffrey Chaucer, the father of English literature, was not shy about including profanity in his works. In 'The Miller's Tale,' one character uses obscene language to describe the cuckolded husband.

Here are some choice examples from this classic text, which was once censored for students forced to study it at school:

Queynte: Chaucer used this term to describe female genitalia in 'The Miller's Tale.' It is a Middle English word that can be seen as a precursor to the modern English word 'quaint.' However, in the context of the tale, it carries a double entendre, suggesting a pun on both its literal and sexual meanings.

Bollen: In 'The Reeve's Tale,' Chaucer uses the word 'bollen' to describe a swollen, distended belly. In the context of the story, it implies that the character's belly is swollen due to overindulgence, which can be seen as a form of gluttony or excess.

Harlotrye: Chaucer uses the term 'harlotrye' in 'The Miller's Tale' to describe promiscuity and infidelity. While the word 'harlot' has evolved to primarily mean a prostitute in modern English, in Chaucer's time, it had a broader meaning that encompassed immoral or promiscuous behavior.

Fart: Chaucer's 'The Summoner's Tale' contains a humorous episode involving a fart. While the word itself may not be considered offensive today, the subject matter and the comedic context are designed to evoke a humorous response from the reader, while it is not clear whether the word is less or more ruder for Chaucer than it may be considered today amongst the more gentile.

Pisse: Chaucer occasionally used words like 'pisse' to refer to urination. While the term itself is not particularly shocking, its directness and the act it describes would have been considered less decorous in certain contexts.

Lechour: In 'The Miller's Tale,' Chaucer uses 'lechour' to describe a man who is a lustful or promiscuous womanizer. This term reflects societal attitudes towards extramarital affairs and sexual indiscretions during Chaucer's time.

The Importance of Early Taboos and Their Modern Relevance

In the grand scheme of history, early taboos surrounding language may seem quaint or even laughable. However, they played a crucial role in shaping societal norms, values, and communication.

Reflection of Society: Early taboos provide us with a mirror to the values and priorities of the societies that upheld them. They reveal what was considered sacred, profane or offensive at different points in history.

Linguistic Evolution: The evolution of language and the changing nature of taboos highlight the dynamic and adaptable nature of human communication. Language is not static; it evolves alongside culture and society.

Cultural Sensitivity: Understanding early taboos can help us appreciate the cultural sensitivities of different eras and regions. It reminds us that what may be offensive today could have been accepted or even celebrated in the past.

Societal Control: The regulation of language, including the prohibition of certain words, has often been a tool of social control. Recognizing this historical aspect can prompt us to question and challenge contemporary attempts to police language.

Freedom of Expression: The struggle against language taboos has been intertwined with the fight for freedom of expression. As societies have grown more tolerant and open, individuals have sought the freedom to express themselves without fear of censorship or punishment.

In our modern world, where freedom of speech is celebrated and linguistic boundaries are constantly tested, early taboos still echo through our language and culture. They remind us that the power of words, both sacred and profane, reflects the ever-evolving human spirit, a testament to our capacity for rebellion, creativity and communication.

So as we continue our journey through the history of swear words, let us keep in mind the ancient taboos that have shaped our language and society. Let us explore the shifting sands of linguistic norms, and may we do so with a sense of curiosity and empathy, for in the world of language and taboo, there is much to learn, much to unlearn and much to ponder.

Chapter 3:
Old English and Middle English Swears

If we are to embark on a journey through the annals of profanity, we must first set our course upon the turbulent seas of antiquity. In this chapter, we shall cast our gaze upon the Old English and Middle English periods, an age where the roots of our modern profanities lie buried beneath the pages of history.

The Genesis of Old English Swears

To understand the origins of swear words in Old English, we must journey back to the time of the Anglo-Saxons, a people whose speech was as rugged as their lifestyles. Their language, Old English, was a Germanic tongue filled with words that could sing like birdsong or rattle like the thunderous clash of swords.

In this era, profanities were closely linked to the physical and the visceral – the tangible experiences of life in an untamed world. They spoke of bodily functions, the scatological and the earthy. Take, for example, the Old English word 'scite,' which referred to feces, or 'stincan,' which meant to stink. These words were blunt, unapologetic and rooted in the gritty realities of existence.

The Usage of Old English Swears

Old English swear words served a multifaceted purpose in their society. They were not merely linguistic transgressions but carried weight and significance, both in daily life and culture.

Catharsis: In the harsh and unforgiving world of the Anglo-Saxons, where life was a battle against nature's whims, profanities offered catharsis. They were a means of releasing pent-up frustration, anger, or pain. The satisfaction of uttering a well-placed expletive after a misstep or an injury was an emotional balm.

Social Stratification: Profanities in Old English were also reflective of social stratification. The nobility and the clergy, bound by decorum and piety, typically refrained from the use of coarse language. It was among the common folk and in the alehouses that swear words found their home, acting as a linguistic divide between classes.

Taboos and Offenses: Old English profanities often dealt with taboo subjects, including sex and bodily functions. Uttering such words could be deeply offensive, as they transgressed the boundaries of modesty and decency upheld by the society.

Here are some examples:

Scite (Shit): Old English had its own term for excrement, similar to the modern English word 'shit.' Discussing bodily waste was considered impolite and offensive.

Fic (Fuck): The word 'fic' in Old English had a similar meaning to the modern English profanity 'fuck,' referring to sexual intercourse. It was considered offensive and was likely used cautiously.

Pyssian (Piss): The Old English term 'pyssian' referred to urination, and explicit discussions about bodily functions like this were considered impolite.

Flaisce (Fart): Farting, like in many cultures, was a topic associated with humor and embarrassment, making explicit discussions about it socially inappropriate.

Searu (Semen): References to semen or sexual fluids were typically avoided in polite conversation, as they related to intimate matters.

Scætan (Defecate): A term related to bowel movements, discussing this bodily function explicitly would have been considered indecent.

Cunnan (Female Genitalia): The Old English word 'cunnan' was associated with female genitalia, and explicit references to it would have been considered taboo.

Dreorig (Bloody): The word 'dreorig' could be associated with violence or bloodshed, and explicit mentions of such topics might have been seen as offensive.

Eccean (Vulva): Similar to references to female genitalia, discussions involving the term 'eccean' would have been regarded as impolite.

Giccan (Itch): The term 'giccan' referred to itching, but in a broader sense, discussions about discomfort or irritation could be seen as offensive.

Brogan (Excrement): Brogan was a term related to feces, and explicit conversations about this bodily waste were likely avoided.

The Evolution of Middle English Swears

As time flowed like a meandering river, Old English evolved into Middle English, carrying with it the legacy of profanities. The Norman Conquest of 1066 brought

French influences and added new dimensions to the language, blending the Old English swears with the refined expressions of the Norman conquerors.

In this era, Middle English swear words began to exhibit a duality – a curious amalgamation of the crass and the cultured. Words like 'queynte' (a euphemism for female genitalia) and 'fart' (an old word for flatulence) coexisted with the more decorous language of the aristocracy.

The Usage of Middle English Swears

Middle English swear words, much like their Old English predecessors, played a significant role in society, albeit in an ever-evolving context:

Bawdy Humor: Middle English profanities often manifested as bawdy humor. Writers and poets of the time, such as Geoffrey Chaucer, reveled in double entendre and innuendo. Chaucer's 'The Miller's Tale,' for example, features humor and wordplay related to sexual themes (as mentioned in the previous chapter).

Social Commentary: Profanities in Middle English could also be a vehicle for social commentary and satire. Writers used explicit language to critique societal norms and behaviors, providing both entertainment and insight.

Cultural Blending: The Norman Conquest introduced new linguistic elements into Middle English, resulting in a language that blended the earthy and the refined. The coexistence of Old English and Norman influences contributed to the complexity of language.

Then there were plenty of oaths like 'God-a-mercy,' 'Od's pitterkins' 'mercy on,' all of which invoked the deity. There were also a-religious oaths such as 'by my beard,' 'by the north pole' and 'a pox on it.'

The Importance of Old and
Middle English Swears

The Old and Middle English periods were crucibles of linguistic evolution, where the foundations of modern English were laid. Profanities in these times were more than mere words; they were the reflection of societal norms, class distinctions and the evolving complexities of human expression.

As we traverse these linguistic epochs, let us not merely revel in the ribaldry of the past but also appreciate the enduring power of language to shape and reflect culture. The swears of Old and Middle English may seem distant and quaint, but they are the ancestors of the colorful language that enriches our modern lexicon.

In the chapters that follow, we shall delve deeper into the labyrinthine corridors of profanity, exploring the nuances and narratives woven into the fabric of words that society has loved, loathed, and laughed at.

23

Chapter 4:
The Renaissance and the Birth of Modern Swearing

The Renaissance stands as a pivotal moment – a time when the echoes of antiquity whispered through the corridors of culture, and the world began to rediscover the power of words. It was an era of rebirth, renewal and yes, the revival of some remarkably inventive forms of swearing.

The Birth of Modern Swearing in Renaissance England

In the fertile soil of Renaissance England, where the English language blossomed under the quills of Shakespeare and Marlowe, swear words took on a new vitality. The era, characterized by its artistic and intellectual ferment, found expression not only in poetry and theater but also in the colorful language of the common folk.

Theatrical Profanity: The English Renaissance theater was a hotbed of linguistic creativity. Playwrights like William Shakespeare and Christopher Marlowe injected their works with irreverent language. In 'King Lear,' for instance, the character Kent employs a blend of creative insults to berate Oswald, Shakespeare's version of the quintessential pompous servant:

Kent: 'I do not like thee, Dr. Fell: the reason why I cannot tell; But this I know, I know full well, I do not like thee, Dr. Fell.'

The reference to 'Dr. Fell' in this context was a clever play on words, using a pseudonym to mock someone.

Oaths and Blasphemy: The religious landscape of Renaissance England was a complex of beliefs and denominations. Swearing often took the form of oaths and blasphemy, reflecting the tension between the Catholic and Protestant worlds. Such language often invoked divine elements and could be especially potent in its offense.

Shakespearean Insults: Shakespeare, the bard of bawdy humor and eloquent vituperation, delighted in inventing imaginative insults. In *Henry IV, Part 1*, Falstaff hurls an iconic insult at Prince Hal:

Falstaff: 'Thou whoreson, obscene, greasy tallow-catch!'

This insult is a delightful mix of vivid imagery and derogatory language, demonstrating Shakespeare's linguistic prowess.

The Renaissance Swearing in France

In France, the Renaissance witnessed its own linguistic flowering. The French language, known for its elegance, found room for profanity amidst its refined vocabulary:

Rabelaisian Ribaldry: François Rabelais, a towering figure of French Renaissance literature, was celebrated for his earthy and satirical humor. In his work 'Gargantua and Pantagruel,' he created a inventive landscape of creative wordplay.

Bawdy Ballads: French ballads and songs of the time often featured explicit language, which added a touch of irreverence to the refined courts of the aristocracy. The famous 'Song of Roland' included colorful language and vulgar themes.

The Renaissance Swearing in Germany

In the heartland of the Holy Roman Empire, the German language offered its own contributions to the world of swearing during the Renaissance:

Scatological Humor: The German language, known for its compound words and linguistic precision, didn't shy away from the scatological. Swear words and expressions often touched on bodily functions and the earthy aspects of life.

Folk Poetry: Folk poetry and songs, often passed down through generations, contained their fair share of explicit language. These works provided a glimpse into the vernacular culture of the time.

The Renaissance Swearing in Italy

In the land of art, literature, and the Renaissance itself, Italy was no stranger to the colorful use of language:

Carnival and Festivals: Italian carnivals and festivals were renowned for their exuberance and revelry. During these celebrations, language took on a licentious and irreverent character, reflecting the spirit of merriment and subversion.

Commedia dell'Arte: The Italian theater tradition of Commedia dell'Arte featured stock characters known for their witty repartee and saucy language. The character Arlecchino (Harlequin), for instance, often engaged in wordplay and bawdy humor.

Famous Examples and Their Stories

William Shakespeare: As the most celebrated playwright of the English Renaissance, Shakespeare's works are replete with inventive language. His insult-laden exchanges, such as those in 'Much Ado About Nothing' or 'Romeo and Juliet,' have become iconic in the world of literature.

François Rabelais: Rabelais, a French Renaissance writer, is best known for his humorous and satirical series 'Gargantua and Pantagruel.' His works brimmed with earthy and inventive language, often used to criticize the follies of his time.

The Notorious François Villon: François Villon, a French poet of the 15th century, was not only celebrated for his verse but also infamous for his run-ins with the law. His poetry, including works like 'The Testament,' featured explicit language and themes of debauchery.

The Legacy of Renaissance Swearing

The Renaissance era was a cauldron of linguistic creativity and cultural upheaval. Swear words of this period were a reflection of society's evolving norms, its conflicts, and its irreverent spirit. In the works of Shakespeare, Rabelais and others, we find not only profanity but also profound insight into the human condition.

As we journey through the annals of history, let us remember that the birth of modern swearing was more than just a cacophony of expletives; it was the dawn of linguistic innovation, cultural critique and a celebration of the boundless power of words. In the chapters ahead, we shall continue our exploration of the profane, the humorous, and the thought-provoking, for in the world of swearing, as in the Renaissance itself, there is always more than meets the ear.

Chapter 5: The Victorian Era: Politeness and Prudishness

Ah, the Victorian era, a time when society was bound by corsets and conventions, when the very mention of a leg, let alone a word, was considered scandalous. In this chapter, we shall delve into the intricacies of swearing during the 19th century, an era of politeness, prudishness and paradoxical profanities.

The Brittle World of 19th-Century Swearing

England, during Queen Victoria's long and prosperous reign, was a land of impeccable manners and stiff upper lips. Swearing, much like the gentlemen and ladies of the time, was expected to be discreet and reserved. But, my dear reader, we humans have always had a penchant for linguistic innovation, especially when the boundaries of politeness tried to keep us in check.

Innovations in Swearing

As language evolved, so did the art of swearing. The 19th century witnessed linguistic creativity, giving rise to new euphemisms and expressions. It was a time when people carefully skirted the line between decency and impropriety.

Victorian Euphemisms: The Victorians excelled in crafting euphemisms to replace more explicit language. Consider phrases like 'the oldest trick in the book' or 'not my cup of tea,' which were used to replace cruder expressions.

Mock Politeness: Another clever innovation was mock politeness. People would use polite-sounding words to mask their true meaning. An exclamation like 'Well, I never!' could carry an undercurrent of disbelief or astonishment.

Indirectness: Victorians often resorted to indirect language to convey their sentiments. A phrase like 'He's rather peculiar' might imply something far less charitable.

Dr. Alex Aaronson

The Context of Swearing in Victorian England

In the prim and proper society of Victorian England, the context of swearing was of utmost importance. Swearing in polite company was frowned upon, but within the privacy of one's own quarters or among close friends, the rules might relax.

Social Class and Swearing: The use of swear words was often tied to one's social class. The working class might employ more colorful language, while the upper classes maintained an air of refinement.

Literary and Artistic Expression: Despite the prudishness of the era, literature and art occasionally explored explicit themes. The works of authors like Oscar Wilde and the artistic movements of the time, such as the Pre-Raphaelites, pushed the boundaries of what was acceptable.

Suppression and Punishment

The Victorian era was marked not only by linguistic innovation but also by concerted efforts to suppress swearing and obscenities. The authorities were keen on maintaining decorum, and there were consequences for those who transgressed.

Obscenity Laws: Various obscenity laws were in place to regulate the use of explicit language in literature and public discourse. Writers like Gustave Flaubert and Oscar Wilde found themselves entangled in legal battles over their works.

Society for the Prevention of Swearing: Yes, such a society existed! The Society for the Prevention of Swearing was founded in the late 19th century, with the noble mission of curbing the use of profanities. It's unclear how successful they were, but one can imagine their meetings were not devoid of irony.

Historical References and Individuals

Let us not forget the colorful characters and incidents that left their mark on the history of swearing during the Victorian era:

Lady Hester Stanhope: This intrepid traveler and adventurer was known for her colorful language and fiery spirit. She once exclaimed, 'May your tea be sweet and your curse words salty!' A fine sentiment indeed.

Lewis Carroll: The author of *Alice's Adventures in Wonderland* and *Through the Looking-Glass* was known for his wordplay and linguistic inventiveness. He often used whimsical language to create humor and nonsense.

The Great French *Dictionnaire Infernal*: This 19th-century compendium of demons and devils featured not only descriptions of infernal beings but also a lexicon of profanities and obscenities. It seems the underworld had its own lexicon of choice words.

The Global Perspective

As we turn our gaze beyond the British Isles, we find that the Victorian era had a significant impact on swearing and censorship in other parts of the world.

France: The French authorities were vigilant in censoring explicit content, and authors like Gustave Flaubert faced legal battles over their works. However, the French are renowned for their creativity in finding euphemisms and playful language.

Germany: German literature of the time often explored taboo subjects, with authors like Heinrich Heine and Johann Nestroy using satire and humor to critique society.

Italy: Italian literature in the 19th century saw authors like Giovanni Verga and Gabriele D'Annunzio addressing explicit themes, albeit within the constraints of societal norms.

Japan and Asia: The Victorian era had a limited direct impact on Japan and other Asian regions. However, cultural norms and censorship influenced the use of explicit language, with the emphasis on politeness and propriety.

In the pages of history, the Victorian era stands as a paradox – a time of both linguistic innovation and suppression, a period where polite society and colorful language coexisted in an intricate dance. As we continue our journey through the annals of profanity, let us savor the inventive euphemisms and the audacity of those who dared to challenge the boundaries of decorum. For, in the world of swearing, even the prim and proper must occasionally let slip a choice word or two, and in doing so, they reveal a truth about the human spirit – that it can never be entirely tamed by the constraints of etiquette and prudery.

Here are a few euphemisms to conjure with:

Leg of the Mutton: A discreet way to refer to a woman's shapely leg, particularly in a flattering or flirtatious context.

Intimate Apparel: Used to describe undergarments, such as corsets, chemises and bloomers, without explicitly mentioning them.

Fancy Man: A term used to refer to a woman's secret lover or paramour.

Conversational Murders: A reference to topics of discussion that were considered off-limits in polite society, particularly those related to bodily functions or sexual matters.

Threading a Needle: A veiled reference to sexual intercourse, with the needle representing a man's member and the threading signifying penetration.

Marital Duties: A genteel way of referring to sexual relations within a marriage, highlighting the expectation of conjugal intimacy.

Special Friends: A euphemism for a close and possibly intimate relationship, often used to describe individuals of the same sex who were romantically involved.

Tea and Toasting: A seemingly innocent reference to a late-night rendezvous involving tea and toasting, which might imply more intimate activities (like today's Netflix and chill).

Walking Out: A Victorian term for courting or dating, suggesting a romantic relationship that may or may not have been formalized. Rather like todays use of the word 'dating.'

Playing the Piano: A metaphor for a woman's self-gratification, with the piano keys symbolizing her intimate areas.

Morning Call: A euphemism for a visit from a woman's monthly menstrual cycle, as discussing such matters openly was considered immodest.

Private Theatricals: A genteel way of referring to intimate or romantic playacting between couples, suggesting amorous role-playing.

Taking Tea: Having sex.

Boudoir Photography: Porn.

Devotion to the Arts: A subtle reference to the sensual or erotic aspects of a romantic relationship.

The Gentleman Caller: A discreet way of referring to a man who frequently visits a woman's home for romantic purposes.

Tête-à-Tête in the Boudoir: To have sex.

Late-Night Poetry Reading: Ditto

The Fireside Chat: Ditto

Nocturnal Revels: Ditto

Behind Closed Curtains: Ditto

Chapter 6:
World War I and the
Soldier's Vocabulary

In the cacophonous theater of war, where the clatter of bullets and the thunder of cannons competed with the cries of men, profanity became a symphony of its own. World War I, with its muddy trenches and relentless horrors, bore witness to a surge in soldierly language, a linguistic battleground that transcended borders and cultures. In this chapter, we shall traverse the minefields of expletives and explore the colorful swearing among English, French, German and American soldiers during the Great War.

The Birth of Soldierly Language

In the trenches of World War I, where life was cheap, death was plentiful, and the camaraderie of soldiers was a fragile shield against the horrors of modern warfare, profanity emerged as a form of coping mechanism, a defiant act against the grim reality of the battlefield.

English Soldiers:
Creative and Colorful

The English soldiers, renowned for their wit and stiff upper lips, exhibited a flair for creative profanity. The British vernacular, already rich with colorful expressions, saw a flourishing of linguistic inventiveness on the front lines.

The Tommy's Language: English soldiers, commonly referred to as 'Tommy Atkins,' coined phrases like 'Blighty' (referring to England) and 'whiz-bang' (a nickname for German artillery shells). These terms were not always profane, but they demonstrated the soldier's ability to adapt and reshape language in the direst of circumstances.

The Somme and 'Oh, Fiddlesticks': The Battle of the Somme in 1916, with its staggering casualties, was a crucible of soldierly language. One anecdote tells of an English soldier responding to the cataclysmic bombardment with an understated,

'Oh, fiddlesticks.' This display of British restraint amid chaos is a testament to their unique brand of humor.

French Soldiers: Mots Crus et Poésie

The French soldiers, known for their poetic sensibilities, mingled the profane with the profound, creating a unique blend of soldierly language.

'Mots Crus': The French possessed a category of profanity known as 'mots crus' or 'raw words.' These were the expletives that peppered their speech on the battlefield, unapologetic in their bluntness.

'La Guerre des Poilus': The soldiers, affectionately called 'poilus' (hairy ones), found solace in writing poetry and letters to loved ones. These compositions often contrasted the brutality of war with the tenderness of their words, showcasing the duality of their linguistic expression.

German Soldiers: Efficiency and Expletives

For the disciplined German soldiers, known for their precision and efficiency, profanity was a release valve for the immense pressure of combat.

'Kriegssprache': The Germans had their own brand of soldierly language, referred to as 'Kriegssprache' (war language). This dialect, which often included profanity, served as a means of communication and camaraderie among soldiers.

'Saukerl' and 'Esel': Commonly used German insults included 'Saukerl' (swine) and 'Esel' (donkey). These derogatory terms could be directed at enemy combatants or fellow soldiers in moments of frustration.

American Soldiers: Yanks and Yelling

The American soldiers, known as 'Yanks,' brought their own brand of swearing to the Western Front, a mixture of homegrown slang and borrowed expressions.

'Son of a Gun': American soldiers often used the phrase 'son of a gun' to express frustration or surprise. While not explicit, it conveyed their emotions vividly.

'Boche': The derogatory term 'Boche' was used by American soldiers to refer to the Germans. It was derived from the French word 'caboche,' meaning head, and was a common expression of disdain.

Famous Incidents and Historical Figures

Throughout World War I, there were notable instances of swearing and colorful language that have left their mark on history.

Sassoon's Poetry: The British poet and soldier Siegfried Sassoon, known for his poignant war poetry, often used explicit language to convey the horrors of war. His poem 'The Kiss' contains stark language that contrasts the brutality of combat with the tenderness of human connection.

The Christmas Truce: During the Christmas Truce of 1914, soldiers from opposing sides exchanged greetings, sang carols, and even played football in no-man's-land. The contrast between the camaraderie of the truce and the brutality of war inspired many soldiers to use colorful language to describe the absurdity of their situation.

Conclusion: A Linguistic Trench Warfare

In the crucible of World War I, where life and death hung in the balance and camaraderie was a lifeline, soldierly language served as a release valve, a coping mechanism and a testament to the resilience of the human spirit. Swearing, in its many forms and languages, became a linguistic trench warfare – a battleground of words and emotions.

As we reflect on the expletives and expressions of English, French, German and American soldiers, let us remember that in the crucible of war, words – however colorful or crude – were a means of preserving sanity, camaraderie, and humanity amidst the chaos and devastation of the Great War. May we, in our exploration of history's linguistic battlefields, find both humor and humility, for in the realm of soldierly language, there is much to learn about the human capacity for expression and resilience.

A list of Tommy curses from WW1. It seems hard to believe in this age that what are now such mild profanities were harsh words amongst the carnage:

Blighter: A term used to refer to someone in a derogatory or humorous manner, often applied to individuals who were disliked or annoying.
Bleedin': An intensifier added to swear words for emphasis. For example, 'bleedin' idiot' or 'bleedin' awful.'

Bally: A mild expletive used for emphasis, similar to 'bloody.' It was often used in phrases like 'bally awful' or 'bally nonsense.'

Bloody: A versatile and commonly used word for emphasis or as an exclamation. It's still used in British English today, though it may not be considered particularly offensive.

Blast: Used as a mild expletive to express frustration or annoyance. Soldiers might exclaim 'blast it' when things didn't go their way.

Bollocks: This term referred to testicles and was used both literally and figuratively. It could be used to criticize something as nonsense or as a profanity expressing disdain.

Bugger: A term used to refer to a sodomite or someone who engages in anal intercourse. It was also used as a general exclamation of frustration or annoyance.

Damn: A mild curse word used to express anger or frustration. Soldiers might say 'damn it' when facing difficulties or setbacks.

Hell: Another versatile exclamation used to convey surprise, anger or frustration. Soldiers might exclaim 'what the hell' when confronted with something unexpected.

Blooming: Similar to 'bloody,' 'blooming' was used for emphasis. Soldiers might say 'blooming awful' to describe a particularly bad situation.

Sod: A shortened form of 'sodomite,' 'sod' was used to refer to a contemptible person. Soldiers might call someone a 'sod' in moments of frustration.

Ruddy: Similar to 'bloody' and 'blooming,' 'ruddy' was used for emphasis. Soldiers might say 'ruddy awful' to express strong disapproval.

Cor Blimey: A euphemistic expression, possibly derived from 'God blind me.' It was used as an exclamation of surprise or amazement, and it played a role in the soldiers' colorful language.

Chapter 7:
The Roaring Twenties:
Flappers and Flirting with
Taboo

Ah, the Roaring Twenties – a time when society donned its finest sequins, jazz filled the air, and rebellion against the stuffy norms of the past was all the rage. But beneath the glitter and glamour of this exuberant era, a linguistic revolution was brewing. In this chapter, we shall shimmy our way through the smoky speakeasies and bustling boulevards of the 1920s in England and America, where swearing took on a new rhythm, and taboos were flirted with like a well-dressed flapper at a clandestine soirée.

The Jazz Age and its Linguistic Swing

The Roaring Twenties was a period of seismic social change, and the language of the time reflected the shifting cultural landscape. As the jazz age swung into high gear, so did the vernacular, and swearing found itself in the spotlight.

England's Rebellious Riposte

In the UK, the 1920s were marked by a rising spirit of rebellion, particularly among the younger generation. The aftermath of World War I and the changing role of women were catalysts for a linguistic evolution.

The Modern Woman: The emergence of the 'flapper' – a young woman who embraced independence, short skirts and social liberation – was a driving force behind linguistic change. These modern women challenged traditional gender roles and, with it, traditional language.

The 'Bright Young Things': London's high-society partygoers, known as the 'Bright Young Things,' were at the forefront of linguistic innovation. They reveled in subverting social norms, and their slang was peppered with risqué terms and wordplay:

Bolshie: A term derived from 'Bolshevik,' 'bolshie' was used to describe someone who was confrontational, defiant, or rebellious.

Giggle Water: A humorous term for alcoholic beverages, reflecting the exuberance of the speakeasy culture.

Roly-Poly: Used to describe someone who was a bit on the heavy side, it was a playful way of poking fun at body shapes.

America's Jazzed-Up Vernacular

Across the pond, America was undergoing its own linguistic transformation. The prohibition era gave rise to a flourishing underground culture, and the language of the speakeasies flowed like bootlegged gin.

Speakeasies and Slang: In the United States, the prohibition of alcohol created a demand for hidden bars known as 'speakeasies.' Here, patrons spoke a language all their own. Phrases like 'bee's knees' (meaning excellent) and 'giggle water' (referring to alcohol) added a playful twist to everyday conversation.

'Flaming Youth': The 1920s saw the rise of the 'flapper,' akin to her British counterpart. She reveled in her newfound freedoms, bobbed her hair, and used slang like 'cat's pajamas' (referring to something excellent) or 'whoopee' (meaning a good time or sex).

Famous Faces and
Their Choice Words

Throughout the 1920s, prominent figures in both England and America contributed to the evolution of language.

Dorothy Parker: The sharp-witted American writer and critic Dorothy Parker was known for her acerbic humor. She once quipped, 'If all the girls who attended the Yale prom were laid end to end, I wouldn't be a bit surprised.'

Noël Coward: The English playwright and composer Noël Coward had a knack for clever wordplay. He famously remarked, 'Wit ought to be a glorious treat like caviar; never spread it about like marmalade.'

Evelyn Waugh: The British novelist Evelyn Waugh, in his book 'Vile Bodies,' provided a humorous glimpse into the slang of the Bright Young Things. His characters reveled in linguistic eccentricities that mirrored the social extravagances of the era.

The Swearing Soirees

Swearing during the Roaring Twenties was as much about playful provocation as it was about linguistic innovation. Parties and gatherings became veritable 'swearing soirees' where guests would exchange the latest risqué phrases and revel in their audacity.

Conclusion: A Linguistic Foxtrot

The Roaring Twenties, with its jazz, flappers and cultural rebellion, marked a turning point in the evolution of language. Swearing and slang flourished as society cast aside Victorian prudishness in favor of bold, irreverent expressions. The lexicon of the time was a linguistic foxtrot, where every step was a dance with taboo.

As we reflect on this era of linguistic liberation, may we appreciate the audacity and creativity that characterized the language of the Roaring Twenties. In a world that was shaking off the shackles of tradition, swearing became an art form, a form of rebellion and a reflection of the times. So, let us raise a toast to the flappers, the Bright Young Things and the jazz age linguists who danced on the edge of propriety, leaving their mark on the words we use today.

The Top Three Swears: No 3

Hold on for a minute. Let's take a breather.

There are three big profanities in the English language. So lets drill on down and look at the history.

In at number 3:

Shit

The word 'shit' is one of the most versatile and frequently used profanities in the English language, with a history that stretches back centuries. Its etymological journey is a fascinating and often colorful tale that reflects the evolution of the English language and its interaction with other cultures. To fully understand the word 'shit,' we need to explore its roots, transformations, and the societal factors that influenced its development.

Old English and Proto-Germanic Origins: The origins of 'shit' can be traced back to the Old English word 'scitan' or 'scitte,' which meant to defecate. This word had its roots in Proto-Germanic, where the word 'skit-' or 'sket-' referred to excrement. The early Germanic peoples used this term to describe the act of bodily waste expulsion, and it eventually found its way into Old English.

The Norman Influence: The Norman Conquest of England in 1066 brought with it a significant influence on the English language. The Normans, who spoke a version of Old French, introduced various words and expressions into English, including those related to bodily functions. The Old French word 'merde' was similar in meaning to 'shit,' and it had an impact on the developing language, though it didn't replace the Old English word entirely.

Middle English and Borrowings: During the Middle English period (from the 12th to the 15th century), English underwent significant changes in vocabulary, pronunciation and grammar. This was a time when many French and Latin words were borrowed into English. The word 'shit' coexisted with other terms like 'crap,' 'dung' and 'excrement' during this period.

Shakespearean Usage: William Shakespeare, one of the most influential playwrights and poets in English literature, did not shy away from using profanity in his works. In his play 'King Lear,' for instance, he employed the word 'shit' in a way that was considered vulgar even in his time. This demonstrates that 'shit' was a known and coarse word in the English language during the Elizabethan era.

Colonial America and Slang Development: As English-speaking settlers established colonies in North America, they brought their language and its profanities with them. The word 'shit' continued to evolve in the American context, influenced by regional dialects and the multicultural nature of the colonies. In the United States, it became a slang term for nonsense or something of poor quality, as in, 'That's a load of shit.'

19th Century Vulgarization and Censorship: During the 19th century, there was a growing awareness of the need for social decorum and a concerted effort to sanitize language. As a result, words like 'shit' were often replaced with euphemisms or asterisks in written texts to avoid explicitness. This era also saw the rise of more acceptable terms like 'feces' or 'stool' in formal discourse.

20th Century and Modern Usage: In the 20th century, with the advent of cinema and television, the restrictions on explicit language began to loosen. The word 'shit' regained some of its original coarseness and became more commonly used in casual speech. It also found its place in various idioms and expressions, such as 'shit happens' and 'holy shit,' which conveyed surprise or dismay.

Pop Culture and Globalization: The spread of American pop culture and media around the world during the 20th and 21st centuries contributed to the global recognition of the word 'shit.' It is now widely understood and used in many non-English-speaking countries, often in its original sense or as a profanity.

Linguistic Perspective: From a linguistic perspective, the word 'shit' can be considered a prime example of how language evolves and adapts to cultural changes. Words that were once considered taboo may become less offensive over time, especially in informal contexts. The acceptance and frequency of profanity in a language can vary greatly depending on social norms and generational shifts.

Conclusion

In summary, the word 'shit' has a long and multifaceted etymological history, evolving from its Old English and Proto-Germanic roots through various influences, including the Norman Conquest, Shakespearean usage and colonization. Its journey reflects the dynamic nature of language, societal norms, and the ever-changing character of words. While 'shit' remains a profanity, it has also found its place in contemporary vernacular, demonstrating the adaptability and resilience of the English language.

Chapter 8:
Hollywood and the Censorship Era: The Emergence of Swearing

Ah, Hollywood, the land of dreams, where anything was possible – except, of course, for the utterance of certain words that could make a sailor blush or the showing of two people lying on a bed. The cinema, a medium so enchanting that it whisked audiences away to far-off lands and distant galaxies, was bound by the unyielding chains of censorship. In this chapter, we shall embark on a cinematic journey through the annals of Hollywood, where swearing was a whispered secret and euphemisms were the order of the day.

The Birth of Hollywood and the Code of Silence

Before we delve into the cinematic swear words that tantalized and titillated, let us first set the stage. Hollywood, in its early years, was a wild west of creativity, a burgeoning industry bursting with tales of gangsters, starlets, and dreams. But even amidst this creative frenzy, there were watchful eyes – moral guardians, critics, and censors who believed in the sanctity of the silver screen.

The Hays Code: Enter the Motion Picture Production Code, often referred to as the Hays Code, after its chief enforcer, Will H. Hays. This code, enforced from 1934 to 1968, was a set of guidelines that dictated what could and could not be shown or said in films. Swearing, of course, fell under the 'could not' category.

Self-Censorship: To avoid running afoul of the Hays Code, studios engaged in a bit of self-censorship. Filmmakers had to find creative ways to express emotions and frustrations without uttering explicit words. Enter the era of euphemisms and innuendo.

The Dance of Euphemisms

In a world where certain words were verboten, filmmakers engaged in a dance of euphemisms, employing clever linguistic devices to convey what couldn't be said outright.

Cocktail Era Euphemisms: The 1930s, often referred to as the 'cocktail era,' was a time of glamour, sophistication and veiled language. Characters in films would exclaim, 'Well, I'll be switched!' or 'Jumping Jehoshaphat!' when faced with surprise or frustration.

Double Entendre: Filmmakers reveled in the art of double entendre, where a phrase had a hidden, often risqué, meaning. A character might remark, 'My, you're a tall drink of water,' which, in the language of cinema, was practically a sonnet of seduction.

Innuendo and Suggestion: Hollywood excelled in the art of suggestion. Characters would engage in conversations filled with innuendo, and viewers were left to read between the lines. What couldn't be shown or said explicitly was hinted at with sly smiles and knowing glances.

Famous Faces in a Censored World

Even the most iconic figures of Hollywood had to navigate the labyrinth of censorship. They became maestros of euphemism, using subtlety and wit to convey what couldn't be uttered.

Yet even against this background a silent movie managed to utter a cussword. In the 1925 silent film 'The Big Parade,' directed by King Vidor, there is a famous scene where the character Slim (played by Karl Dane) utters the word 'goddamit' while trying to light a cigarette and in the heat of battle 'bastards'. It was a silent movie but you didn't needed to be a lip reader as there were subtitle cards and 'bastards' became 'b******s.' In the context of the film and the time it was made, this utterance was considered quite a shock, as profanity was strictly regulated in Hollywood during the silent film era. 'The Big Parade' is often cited for its groundbreaking use of language in this scene, as it marked a departure from the usual level of censorship in films of that era. It was a huge box office hit.

Mae West: The inimitable Mae West, a massive box office star, was a master of suggestive dialogue. In the film 'She Done Him Wrong' (1933), she delivered lines like, 'Is that a gun in your pocket, or are you just glad to see me?' with a knowing wink. Many have suggested that was a sexual reference, but it may be a fallacy.

Clark Gable: The legendary Clark Gable, in 'Gone with the Wind' (1939), uttered the famous line, 'Frankly, my dear, I don't give a damn.' The word 'damn' caused quite a stir as the first cussing in a talky but is tame by today's standards. It was a huge box office hit.

Hollywood's Rebel Cry:
Bonnie and Clyde and the F-Bomb

As the decades rolled on, and social norms evolved, Hollywood's restraint began to loosen. The 1960s ushered in a new era of cinema – one that dared to push boundaries and challenge the censorship of old.

Bonnie and Clyde (1967): Directed by Arthur Penn and starring Warren Beatty and Faye Dunaway, this film is often credited with introducing the F-word to mainstream cinema. 'Fuck' was in the script, but not the actual film dialogue; however, the story of a young couple obsessed with sex and violence was to set a new tone. It was a huge box office hit.

It wasn't until 1970's *M*A*S*H* that the F-word was finally heard on screen. It is spoken during the football game near the end of the film by Walt 'Painless Pole' Waldowski when he says to an opposing football player, 'All right, Bud, your fucking head is coming right off!'

The Changing Landscape: these films were a harbinger of change. Hollywood began to embrace a more realistic, unfiltered portrayal of language and life. The Hays Code lost its grip, and the floodgates of profanity gradually opened.

Yet more advancement, Hollywood's flirtation with profanity has never been dull, and one landmark moment deserves a special mention. In the midst of Hollywood's evolving relationship with censorship, the action-packed classic *Die Hard* (1988) directed by John McTiernan and starring Bruce Willis broke new ground. The film featured one of cinema's memorable and liberating utterances of the word 'motherfucker.' John McClane's (Willis) exclamation of 'Yippee-ki-yay, motherfucker!' became an iconic battle cry, symbolizing the shift towards a more audacious use of language in the world of film. 'Die Hard' was a testament to the changing tides in Hollywood, where the language of cinema was no longer confined by the old rules, and where even the most colorful of expressions found its place amidst the action and mayhem. It was, indeed, a cinematic moment that had audiences cheering and censor boards gasping in equal measure. It was a huge box office hit.

While without doubt there have been plenty of 'shit' scripts, the first occurrence of the word in a script appears to be unrecorded.

Conclusion: Lights, Camera, Swear!

In the world of Hollywood, where dreams and reality coalesced on the silver screen, the language was once as meticulously manicured as a starlet's image. But as time marched on, the world grew more complex, and the once-taboo words found their way into scripts and dialogues.

As we look back on this era of cinematic censorship and the emergence of swearing, let us raise our glasses to the actors, writers, and filmmakers who danced on the precipice of propriety. They navigated the labyrinth of euphemisms and double entendre, leaving us with a legacy of creative language that continues to echo in the halls of Hollywood. Swearing, once a whispered secret, emerged as a bold, if occasionally bleeped, form of expression has often been the spicy ingredient added to cook up a blockbuster. So, in the words of Hollywood, 'Cut! Print it!' and let the curtain rise on the next act of our linguistic journey through time.

Chapter 9:
The Post-War Boom –
Changing Social Norms

The post-war era, from 1946 to 1960, was a time of seismic shifts and societal transformation. As the world emerged from the wreckage of World War II, a brave new world was taking shape – one where the staid conventions of the past had being shaken to their core and fractured. In this chapter, we shall traverse the post-war landscape of Britain and America, where the language of swearing underwent a renaissance and old norms found themselves eroding away.

The Winds of Change

As the war-weary populace dusted off their fedoras and poodle skirts, there was a palpable yearning for a fresh start. But change was not always comfortable, and the language of the time reflected this tumultuous period.

The Easing of Censorship: With the cessation of hostilities, the tight grip of wartime censorship began to loosen. Films, radio, and print media were no longer under the same constraints, and the language began to reflect this newfound freedom.

Media Pioneers: Visionaries in the world of media saw an opportunity to push boundaries. Their audacity led to the emergence of new and daring forms of expression.

Old Media, New Rules:
Newspapers and Radio

The post-war era saw the emergence of previously forbidden words and phrases in newspapers and radio broadcasts. This was not without its controversies.

The Lenny Bruce Phenomenon: In the late 1950s and early 1960s, American comedian Lenny Bruce challenged the status quo with his provocative and profanity-laden stand-up routines. His performances often resulted in legal troubles and arrests, as his language was deemed obscene.

The Angry Young Men: British playwrights and authors like John Osborne and Kingsley Amis shook the literary world with their gritty depictions of working-class life. Their works, including 'Look Back in Anger' and 'Lucky Jim,' featured characters who spoke in frank, uncensored language.

The Birth of Rock and Roll: Shaking Things Up

In the realm of music, rock and roll was the revolutionary force that took the world by storm. It wasn't just about catchy tunes; it was also about challenging societal norms, often through euphemisms for sex.

Elvis Presley: The King of Rock and Roll, Elvis Presley, embodied the rebellious spirit of the era. His hip-shaking performances and lyrics broadly hinted at sexuality and were a source of controversy and fascination. Elvis the Pelvis begin a tradition of performance that leads to the twerking of today where simulation has long since replaced suggestion.

Chuck Berry: Chuck Berry's iconic songs, including 'Maybellene' and 'Roll Over Beethoven,' were infused with the energy and language of youth culture. His lyrics resonated with a generation eager to break free from the past while being infused with camouflaged adult themes.

Bill Haley and the Comets: With their hit song 'Rock Around the Clock,' Bill Haley and the Comets signaled a seismic shift in popular music. The catchy tune and exuberant lyrics captured the zeitgeist of the era. Rock quickly became a replacement for another four letter word ending with CK.

The Limits of Acceptability: Comic Books and TV

Comic books and television also grappled with the changing norms of the post-war period. The introduction of new characters and themes pushed the boundaries of what was deemed acceptable.

Comic Books: The emergence of antiheroes and complex characters in comic books challenged traditional depictions of good versus evil. 'Holy hamstrings' characters like Batman and Spider-Man tackled real-world issues and replaced strong language with replacement ejaculations.

Television: The television industry struggled with censorship during this period. Shows like 'All in the Family' dared to address social and political issues, including racism and war, with a level of candor that was groundbreaking.

Famous Examples Across Europe and Britain

As the winds of change swept through Europe and Britain, media across the continent also underwent transformation.

France: Jean-Paul Sartre's play 'No Exit' featured characters engaged in existential debates and used strong language. The play challenged conventional morality and language.

Italy: Federico Fellini's film 'La Dolce Vita' explored the decadence and moral ambiguity of Roman society. It pushed the boundaries of cinematic storytelling and expression.

Britain: The 'angry young men' of British literature, as mentioned earlier, played a pivotal role in challenging societal norms and language in the United Kingdom.

Conclusion: The New Dawn of Swearing

The post-war era was a crucible of change, where the language of swearing underwent a renaissance. Old norms were shattered, and the media became a battleground for societal transformation. From the risqué routines of Lenny Bruce to the revolutionary sound and culture of rock and roll, the post-war period heralded a new dawn of expression.

As we look back on this time of upheaval, let us remember the pioneers and provocateurs who dared to challenge conventions, even at the risk of legal troubles and public outrage. The language of swearing, once stifled, found its voice in the cacophony of change, forever altering the way we communicate and reflect the shifting values of society. In the end, it was a period of audacious exploration, where the words we used reflected the tumultuous journey from the old world to the new.

Chapter 10:
The 1960s – Counterculture and Freedom of Expression

The swinging sixties, a time of groovy tunes, flower power, and a profound cultural shift that swept across both sides of the Atlantic. It was an era that celebrated freedom of expression, and words, once shrouded in taboo, found their voice amidst the counterculture revolution. In this chapter, we shall journey through the tumultuous decade of the 1960s, where swearing broke free from its linguistic chains, and the world would never be the same again.

A Shifting Social Landscape

The 1960s were a decade of transformation and rebellion, a time when societal norms were challenged, and a new cultural landscape emerged. This shift extended to the realm of language and swearing.

Counterculture and the Freedom of Expression: The counterculture movement, with its anti-establishment ethos, embraced freedom of expression as a core principle. This philosophy extended to language, which was no longer confined to the polite constraints of the past.

Psychedelics and Altered States: The use of mind-altering substances, such as LSD, became intertwined with the counterculture movement. These experiences often led to a reevaluation of language and a desire to explore new realms of expression.

Media Mirrors the Zeitgeist: Newspapers and Magazines

The emergence of alternative newspapers and underground magazines provided a platform for writers and artists to push the boundaries of language and expression.

The Underground Press: Publications like *The Village Voice* in the United States and *Oz* in the United Kingdom played a pivotal role in challenging established norms. They featured articles and illustrations that explored previously taboo subjects, including explicit language.

Swearing in Print: Some publications began to use explicit language to reflect the counterculture's rejection of convention. For example, the word 'fuck' started appearing in print frequently, testing the limits of acceptability.

The Televised Revolution: TV and Film

Television and cinema were not immune to the winds of change. The entertainment industry began to reflect the evolving language and attitudes of the era.

The Smothers Brothers Comedy Hour: This American variety show, hosted by Tom and Dick Smothers, was known for its political and social commentary. It often pushed the boundaries of what was considered acceptable on television, including the use of stronger language.

Film and Swearing: Films of the 1960s, such as *Easy Rider* and *Midnight Cowboy*, explored themes of rebellion and nonconformity. They featured characters who used explicit language as a form of defiance, reflecting the counterculture's rejection of traditional norms.

Comic Books and Pop Art

Comic books, initially seen as dangerous, had become bastions of wholesome entertainment, but underwent a transformation in the 1960s. The emergence of pop art and alternative comics challenged the status quo.

Rise of Underground Comics: Alternative and underground comics, including Robert Crumb's *Zap Comix*, broke free from the Comics Code Authority's restrictions. These comics often featured explicit language and content.

Lichtenstein's Influence: Pop artist Roy Lichtenstein's use of onomatopoeic words in his artwork, such as 'Whaam!' and 'Pow!', played with the idea of language as a visual element and challenged traditional artistic norms. While Victorian's might say those words were not 'swear words' they would admit they were textual outburst, and soon enough there would be fine artworks with swear words written on them.

Music and the Psychedelic Soundscape

The music of the 1960s was a powerful catalyst for change, with artists using their lyrics and performances to challenge societal norms and explore new linguistic territories.

The Beatles: The Fab Four's music evolved with the times, and their album *Sgt. Pepper's Lonely Hearts Club Band* featured the line 'It's getting better all the time' in the song *Getting Better*, which marked a subtle acknowledgment of changing attitudes toward language. One iconic example of this shift occurred when The Beatles recorded 'Hey Jude.' Released in 1968, the song featured a fleeting but audible utterance of the word 'fucking' during a tumultuous studio session. Though often debated among fans and scholars, this rare inclusion of explicit language within a Beatles track marked a subtle nod to the evolving norms of the era. It whispered that even the most beloved and mainstream of bands were part of the linguistic revolution of the time.

The Rolling Stones: The Stones' song *Let's Spend the Night Together* was considered scandalous at the time, as the lyrics hinted at sexual encounters. This was an early example of music pushing the boundaries of lyrical content. In the US where 'damn' had long fallen out of contention as a swear word, The Rolling Stones' hit song *Satisfaction* was making waves. Released in 1965, the song featured the phrase 'I can't get no satisfaction' in its chorus. The use of the double negative 'can't get no' was seen by some as a reference to sexual frustration. Radio stations and advertisers raised objections, leading to calls for censorship and even a ban on the song especially for the reference of 'making a girl.' The controversy surrounding *Satisfaction* highlighted the tension between artists pushing the boundaries of expression and the conservative forces seeking to uphold traditional values. It was a moment when language and music collided in a battle over the limits of acceptable lyrical content, mirroring the larger cultural upheaval of the decade. The word 'making' was blanked out in radio, in a similar way 'faggot' has gone missing from *Money For Nothing* by Dire Straits.

Famous Examples Across Europe and America

As the counterculture movement reverberated across Europe and America, media on both continents reflected the changing language and attitudes of the era.

Ulysses: James Joyce's novel *Ulysses* had been banned in several countries for its explicit language and content. In the 1960s, the United States finally lifted the ban, and the novel was legally available.

Last Exit to Brooklyn: Hubert Selby Jr.'s novel *Last Exit to Brooklyn* was a controversial work that pushed the boundaries of explicit language and content. It faced legal challenges but ultimately contributed to changing attitudes toward censorship.

Conclusion:
The Linguistic Revolution

The 1960s were a time of profound cultural transformation, where the counterculture movement celebrated freedom of expression, and language became a vehicle for rebellion and self-expression. From the pages of underground newspapers to the lyrics of rock anthems, swearing and explicit language emerged from the shadows.

As we look back on this era of linguistic revolution, let us remember the pioneers who challenged established norms, pushing the boundaries of language and expression. The 1960s were a time when words were set free, reflecting the seismic shifts in society and culture. It was a decade where the counterculture's rejection of convention was echoed in the language of defiance, forever altering the way we communicate and view the world. In the end, it was a linguistic revolution that embraced the power of words to challenge, inspire, and change the world.

Chapter 11:
The Rise of Stand-Up Comedy and the Swear Words Revolution

In our society where words are both sword and shield, there emerged a peculiar and profound art form known as stand-up comedy. The comedy club stages of America and the pub back rooms of Britain witnessed a revolution that shattered linguistic conventions, transforming the way we laughed, gasped and occasionally winced. In this chapter, we delve into the uproarious world of stand-up comedy and the birth of 'alternative comedy,' exploring how the embrace of swear words became an essential brushstroke on the canvas of humor, both in the United States and the United Kingdom.

The Emergence of Stand-Up Comedy

Before we embark on our comedic journey, let us pay homage to the roots of stand-up comedy, a genre that has tickled our collective funny bone for generations.

Vaudeville and One-Man Shows: Stand-up comedy has its origins in vaudeville and variety shows, where individual performers entertained audiences with monologues, jokes and anecdotes. Vaudeville acts laid the foundation for what would become the modern stand-up routine. The famous comic of the 1940's Mick Miller, a favorite of the then Queen, was banned from the airwaves for a joke where his choices on meeting a naked woman on a narrow bridge were to toss himself off or block the passage. In the modern era this atavistic lewdness is about all that is remembered of him.

Radio and Television: With the advent of radio and television, comedians like Jack Benny and Milton Berle found a new platform for their humor. These pioneers of comedy helped shape the American comedic landscape for years to come.

The Comedy Club Revolution: George Carlin and Lenny Bruce

As the 20th century progressed, stand-up comedy underwent a transformation, thanks to the audacious voices of George Carlin and Lenny Bruce.

George Carlin: The irreverent George Carlin dared to challenge societal norms with his thought-provoking and profanity-laden routines. His famous 'Seven Dirty Words' skit became a battle cry for comedians seeking to push the boundaries of acceptable language, not only in the United States but also inspiring comics across the pond in the United Kingdom.

Lenny Bruce: Lenny Bruce, the enfant terrible of stand-up comedy, was a trailblazer in every sense. His fearless performances confronted censorship and censorship's champions head-on, leading to numerous arrests and legal battles. Bruce's commitment to free speech paved the way for future generations of comedians on both sides of the Atlantic.

The Birth of 'Alternative Comedy' in the UK

As the 1980s dawned, a new wave of comedy emerged in the United Kingdom, bearing the label 'alternative comedy.' It was a reaction against the stale conventions of traditional comedy and found its own unique voice.

The Comedy Store: In London, The Comedy Store became a mecca for alternative comedy, showcasing comedians like Alexei Sayle and Ben Elton. These performers often incorporated explicit language and provocative humor into their acts, challenging the comedic norms of the time.

The Comic Strip: The Comic Strip, a group of comedians from the Comedy Store that included Rik Mayall and Adrian Edmondson, challenged the established comedy order. Their television series and live performances introduced a fresh, irreverent style of comedy that often-featured strong language and taboo-breaking humor.

The Young Ones: The television show *The Young Ones*, created by Ben Elton, Rik Mayall and others, was a riotous celebration of alternative comedy. Its characters reveled in anarchic humor, frequently using swear words and irreverent language to express their disdain for convention.

One of the early instances of swearing on British television can be traced back to the iconic British sitcom *Till Death Us Do Part*, which first aired in 1965. The show was known for its controversial and groundbreaking nature, often featuring the character Alf Garnett, played by Warren Mitchell, using strong and offensive language.

One of the most famous early instances of swearing in the series occurred in the episode titled *Christmas Night with the Stars* in 1966. Alf Garnett used the word 'bloody' in his dialogue, which was considered strong language for TV at the time. While the word 'bloody' might not seem particularly offensive today, in the context of the 1960s, it was a significant departure from the more genteel and restrained language typically used on television.

It's important to note that the use of strong language in *Till Death Us Do Part* was a reflection of the character Alf Garnett's outspoken and bigoted nature. The show was a pioneering example of how television comedy could tackle controversial subjects and use language that was considered taboo at the time to make a point.

Why Swearing Makes Comedy Funnier

The age-old question: Why do we find swear words so funny? There's a curious alchemy at play when it comes to profanity and humor, whether it's on the stages of American comedy clubs or the pubs of British alternative comedy.

Taboo and Surprise: Swear words carry an inherent taboo, and comedy thrives on subverting expectations. When a comedian delivers a well-timed swear word, it often catches the audience off guard, generating surprise and laughter.

Release of Tension: Swearing can serve as a release valve for tension. In the crucible of humor, swear words can punctuate a joke or defuse an awkward moment, inviting the audience to share in the comic's rebellion.

The Power of Authenticity: Swearing can lend authenticity to a comedian's performance. It conveys a sense of raw, unfiltered emotion that resonates with audiences. In a world of scripted politeness, swearing feels refreshingly real.

The Legacy of Laughter and Liberation

As we reflect on the rise of stand-up comedy and the embrace of swear words in humor, let us celebrate the comedians who fearlessly pushed boundaries and challenged the status quo.

Swear words, once relegated to the shadows of social decorum, now dance in the spotlight of comedic expression. They have become the comic's secret weapon, a linguistic dynamite that tickles our sensibilities and unshackles our laughter. In the end, it is through humor, audacity, and the clever use of swear words that these comedic pioneers have etched their names into the annals of comedic history, reminding us that laughter is, indeed, the ultimate liberation, whether in the heart of New York City or the vibrant comedy scene of London.

Chapter 12:
Television and Censorship Battles

Where the airwaves hummed with stories, laughter and drama, there existed a battle that was waged with words and images. It was a battle against censorship, where the boundaries of what could be said and shown were constantly tested. In this chapter, we embark on a journey through the annals of television history in both the United States and the United Kingdom, exploring the emergence of swearing and bad language, the controversies they sparked, and the responses that shaped the medium we know today.

The American Frontier

The Smothers Brothers Comedy Hour (1967-1969)

Our journey into television's censorship battles begins with a comedic duo that dared to challenge the status quo. Tom and Dick Smothers, better known as the Smothers Brothers, brought humor to the forefront of American television with *The Smothers Brothers Comedy Hour*.

The Censorship Clash: The Smothers Brothers were no strangers to controversy, but their skirmish with CBS network censors in 1968 over an episode featuring Harry Belafonte was a defining moment. The use of the word 'hell' in the episode raised eyebrows.

The Outcome: The episode aired with the word 'hell' bleeped out, but it marked the beginning of a series of conflicts between the Smothers Brothers and CBS. Ultimately, the network canceled their show in 1969, citing creative differences. The clash highlighted the power struggle between comedians seeking artistic freedom and network censors.

All in the Family (1971-1979)

Based on the controversial British Comedy *Till Death Us Do Part* in the early 1970s, Norman Lear's 'All *in the Family* made waves with its groundbreaking approach to social issues. The show's central character, Archie Bunker, was a brash and bigoted individual.

The Taboo Episodes: *All in the Family* addressed taboo subjects head-on. In one episode, titled *Edith's 50th Birthday*, Archie Bunker used a racial slur during a heated exchange, pushing the boundaries of acceptable language on television.

The Outcome: The episode aired with the offensive word bleeped out, but it ignited a firestorm of debate and discussion. Norman Lear defended the decision as a way to highlight Archie Bunker's bigotry. The controversy surrounding the episode underscored the power of television to challenge societal norms and spark important conversations.

The British Invasion

Monty Python's Flying Circus (1969-1974)

Across the Atlantic, a group of irreverent comedians known as Monty Python were reshaping the landscape of British comedy with *Monty Python's Flying Circus.*

The Naughty Bits: Monty Python's sketches often featured content that raised eyebrows. The 'Nudge Nudge' sketch, performed by Eric Idle, amplified the sexual innuendo that obsessed the British, leaving audiences in stitches.

The Outcome: While the Pythons faced objections and censorship, their clever use of wordplay and absurdity often allowed them to escape the limits of previous norms. The show became a cultural phenomenon, demonstrating that humor could be both subversive and transcendent.

Spitting Image (1984-1996)

In the 1980s, *Spitting Image* emerged as a satirical puppet show that spared no one in its biting humor, including public figures and celebrities.

The Royal Controversy: In 1986, an episode lampooned the Royal Family, with Princess Anne depicted in a less-than-flattering manner. The depiction led to heated discussions about the limits of satire.

The Outcome: While the show faced occasional controversies and censorship, *Spitting Image* continued to satirize politicians and celebrities with biting humor. It illustrated the power of television to challenge authority and provide a platform for political satire.

Reporting and Backlash

The battles over censorship in television were not confined to the studios and screens alone. They spilled into the pages of newspapers and the voices of critics.

Media Coverage: The clashes over censorship were extensively covered by newspapers, magazines and television programs. They became subjects of national debates and discussions, sparking conversations about the role of television in shaping cultural norms.

Public Response: The battles over censorship often saw public response and backlash. Viewers and advocacy groups weighed in on the debates, with opinions divided along lines of free speech, morality, and artistic expression.

Conclusion: A Shifting Landscape

As we conclude our exploration of television and censorship battles, we are reminded that these battles are not mere skirmishes but reflections of societal change. The victories and defeats in these battles have reshaped the boundaries of television, once again challenging conventional norms and inviting viewers to confront complex questions of art, expression and freedom.

In the annals of television history, these censorship battles are chapters that illuminate the journey of a medium as it matures, evolves and navigates the ever-changing tides of culture. From the Smothers Brothers to Monty Python, from *All in the Family* to *Spitting Image*, the comedians and creators who dared to challenge the status quo left an indelible mark on television's narrative. They reminded us that words have power, and the battle over what can and cannot be said on television continues to shape the stories we tell and the way we tell them. It underlines the potency of the shock of the new and the fascination of the transgressive.

Chapter 13:
Music Lyrics and Parental Advisory Labels

The hills are not just alive with the sound of music, where words meld with melody to create an auditory delight, there exists a rugged landscape marked by a cacophony of rebellion and controversy. It's a horizon that rings with the evolution of lyrics, that morph from subtle innuendo to unabashed swearing, creating a profound impact on both sides of the Atlantic. Join us on this musical odyssey through the United States and the United Kingdom, as we explore the emergence of swear words and explicit language in lyrics, the transformative influence of hip-hop, and how this lyrical revolution rippled through various forms of media, forever altering the creative landscape.

A Prelude to Profanity

Before we dive headlong into the tempestuous waters of explicit lyrics, it's essential to recognize the gentle innuendos and playful metaphors that paved the way for the lyrical audacity that was to follow.

The American Crooners

In the early days of American music, crooners like Bing Crosby and Frank Sinatra held sway over audiences with their suave voices and lyrics that tantalized with subtle suggestions rather than explicit declarations. These artists were masters of the art of the double entendre.

For example, Frank Sinatra's rendition of *I've Got You Under My Skin* is a masterclass in sensuality. The song skillfully conveys desire without resorting to overtly explicit language. While every one was *Making Whoopie* the naïve could interpret that as just having fun, while the more world weary would take it another way. While the 'birds and the bees do it, and even educated flees do it,' children and adults could make of that as they wished.

The British Invasion

Across the pond, the British Invasion brought with it a wave of bands, most notably The Beatles, who cleverly wove suggestive elements into their lyrics. Songs like *A Hard Days Night* swapped innuendo for vagueness, 'where the things that you do,' could make you feel alright.

The brilliance of The Beatles lay in their ability to convey passion and desire through seemingly innocent phrases. 'I want to hold your hand' was a straightforward expression of yearning, yet it resonated deeply with listeners and evoked powerful emotions.

The Emergence of Swear Words

As the 1960s transitioned into the 1970s, a seismic shift in the musical landscape began to take shape. The counterculture was in full swing, and a thirst for authenticity paved the way for more explicit forms of musical expression.

The Rolling Stones and 'Brown Sugar' (1971)

The Rolling Stones, perennial icons of rebellion and rock 'n' roll, found themselves courting controversy with their 1971 hit, *Brown Sugar*. The lyrics of this song delved into sensitive topics, such as slavery, drug use and sexual desire, with an audacity that pushed the boundaries of acceptable content in popular music.

Lines like 'Brown sugar, how come you taste so good, now?' coupled with references to slave trade and sexual innuendos, left little to the imagination. It was a departure from the subtlety of earlier eras and a harbinger of a lyrical revolution that remains controversial to this day.

The Who and 'Who Are You' (1978)

The Who, another legendary British rock band, contributed to the evolution of explicit lyrics with their 1978 hit, 'Who Are You.' In this song, a memorable line stood out: 'Who the fuck are you?' The inclusion of such profanity was a bold statement, and it signaled a departure from the more restrained lyrics of the past.

This explicit line, uttered with swagger and irreverence, hinted at the changing tides of lyrical expression. It was a sign of things to come in the realm of music.

Dr. Alex Aaronson

Hip-Hop's Impact

The 1980s heralded the rise of hip-hop, a genre that would not only reshape the musical landscape but also redefine the use of explicit language in lyrics.

Run-D.M.C. and 'Rock Box' (1984)

Run-D.M.C., one of the pioneers of hip-hop, made a significant impact with their 1984 track, *Rock Box*. What set this song apart was its incorporation of rock elements into hip-hop, creating a fusion that was both innovative and provocative.

In *Rock Box*, Run-D.M.C. combined bold language with vivid storytelling, marking a departure from the subtlety of earlier eras. The lyrics exuded confidence and rebellion, reflecting the ethos of a new generation.

N.W.A. and 'Straight Outta Compton' (1988)

N.W.A. burst onto the scene in 1988 with their groundbreaking album, *Straight Outta Compton*. This seminal work was characterized by unapologetic and explicit language that vividly depicted the harsh realities of urban life, particularly in Los Angeles.

Songs like *Fuck tha Police* and *Straight Outta Compton* were unfiltered expressions of frustration and outrage. They didn't hold back, and their raw honesty resonated with the audience. The album sparked debates about free speech, artistic expression, and the role of music in addressing societal issues.

The Parental Advisory Label

With the surge of explicit lyrics in the 1980s, concerns about their impact on young listeners began to grow. This led to the creation of the Parental Advisory Label, a watershed moment in music history.

The PMRC and Senate Hearings (1985)

The Parents Music Resource Center (PMRC), led by Tipper Gore and other prominent figures, called for warning labels on albums with explicit content. In 1985, Senate hearings brought this issue to the national stage, igniting a fierce debate about the influence of music on youth.

The PMRC's concerns revolved around themes of sex, drugs, violence, and profanity in lyrics. Artists and musicians argued that the labels were a form of censorship that infringed upon their right to free expression.

The Outcome

As a result of the PMRC's efforts, the Recording Industry Association of America (RIAA) introduced the Parental Advisory Label in 1985. Albums featuring explicit content were affixed with a black-and-white sticker, warning parents about the lyrical content.

The introduction of the label marked a pivotal moment in the music industry's history. While it aimed to inform parents about potentially objectionable content, it also raised questions about censorship, artistic freedom, and the role of parental responsibility in regulating their children's music consumption. Many stores refused to stock records that sported the parental advisory sticker, leading to reduced sales for controversial records.

The Influence on Other Media

The impact of explicit lyrics in music extended beyond the realm of sound, reshaping the boundaries of acceptability in various forms of media.

Film and Television

The influence of explicit lyrics in music inspired filmmakers and television creators to push the envelope in their respective mediums. Films like *New Jack City* (1991) and *Boyz n the Hood* (1991) explored themes of urban life, drugs, and violence, often featuring soundtracks that echoed the explicit language found in hip-hop lyrics.

On television, series like *The Sopranos* (1999-2007) featured complex characters who freely used explicit language, mirroring the gritty realism of hip-hop. These portrayals challenged traditional television norms and contributed to the evolving landscape of televised content.

Comedy

Comedy, too, felt the reverberations of the lyrical revolution in music. Comedians like Richard Pryor and Eddie Murphy, incorporated explicit language into their stand-up routines. These comedians pushed the boundaries of what was considered acceptable on stage, using humor to address societal issues identity, and personal experiences.

Conclusion: A Lyrical Revolution

As we conclude our journey through the world of music lyrics and the influence of explicit language, we are reminded that music has always been a mirror reflecting the evolving norms and values of society. From the subtle innuendos of crooners to the unapologetic swagger of hip-hop, lyrics have been a medium for artists to express their truths, confront social issues, and challenge the status quo.

The emergence of swear words and explicit language in lyrics marked a departure from the restrained norms of the past. It was a lyrical revolution that resonated with audiences, sparking debates about free speech, censorship and the responsibility of artists.

The introduction of the Parental Advisory Label signaled a new era in the music industry, acknowledging the need for transparency while raising questions about artistic freedom. It was a reminder that music, like any art form, has the power to influence culture and provoke thought. It also rode the age old marketing wave that nothing is more juicy than forbidden fruit.

The influence of explicit lyrics in music extended beyond its auditory realm, shaping the narratives of films, television series and stand-up comedy. It challenged traditional boundaries and encouraged a more honest and unfiltered approach to storytelling.

In this lyrical revolution, music became a vessel for artists to express themselves authentically, addressing the complexities of life in the modern world. It was a journey marked by controversy, but it also marked a transformation in the way we perceive and engage with the art of sound and language.

Chapter 14:
Profanity in Literature and Poetry

Where words unfurl like banners and emotions surge through the symphony of language, there exists a chapter shrouded in darkness – a chapter that dares to explore the forbidden alleys of profanity, swearing, and the unbridled power of words in literature and poetry. In this chapter, we journey through the annals of English literature from the 18th century to the present day, unveiling the emergence, progression and pivotal moments in the use of profanity. Join us as we traverse the landscape of audacity, examining the firsts, stories and outcomes that have left an indelible mark on the world of letters.

A Prelude to Profanity

Before we plunge headlong into the depths of literary and poetic profanity, let's pause to acknowledge the subtle whispers and restrained expressions that quietly set the stage for what was to come. Ancient poets such as Catullus and Sappho were sometimes considered obscene because of their graphic depictions of sexual acts.

But first let's get to the first four letter poem.

The earliest known published use of the word 'fuck' in a poem can be traced back to a poem titled *Flen flyys*, which is part of a collection known as the *Harley Lyrics*. These lyrics date back to the 15th century, during the Middle English period. The poem contains the line:

'fvccant vvivys of heli'

In this line, 'fvccant' is a variant spelling of 'fuck,' and 'vvivys' is a variant spelling of 'wives.' The line can be roughly translated as 'fuck the wives of hell.' It also states 'Swyve þu so deþ.' a modern translation of which can be parsed as 'Have sex as if it's your last.'

The *Harley Lyrics*, also known as the Harley Manuscript or Harley 2253, is a medieval English manuscript dating back to the late 15th century. Housed in the British Library, it contains a collection of secular and religious poetry, songs, carols, and other texts. Among these writings, the Harley Lyrics stand out as a fascinating glimpse into the language and culture of the period.

The lyrics showcase a wide range of themes, from courtly love to religious devotion. They provide insights into the linguistic evolution of Middle English and the poetic forms popular at the time. The inclusion of explicit language and themes in some poems reflects the less rigid standards of the era. These lyrics continue to be of interest to scholars and enthusiasts studying medieval literature and culture, shedding light on the diverse expressions of the human experience during the late Middle Ages.

The Restoration Era (1660-1688)

Amid the chaotic backdrop of the English Restoration, a period of profound social and political transformation, literature began to flirt with themes that would later evolve into profanity. John Wilmot, the 2nd Earl of Rochester, was among the literary provocateurs of the era. His bawdy and irreverent poetry, including works like *The Imperfect Enjoyment* (1670), dared to explore the boundaries of desire and sexuality with a daring audacity that foreshadowed the turbulence of the future.

Here is a list of some works from the period that would have got the pulse racing:

L'École des Filles (The School for Girls) by Michel Millot (c. 1668) – This French erotic book is known for its explicit content and illustrations, often focusing on sexual education for women.

The School of Venus by Anonymous (c. 1680) – Another erotic work, this English text is designed as an educational dialogue on sexual matters.

The Country Good Advice for the Eminent City Dame by Aphra Behn (1684) – Aphra Behn was one of the first professional female writers in English literature, and her work often explored sexual themes. This satirical pamphlet mocks the city life and offers ribald advice.

Lust's Dominion by Christopher Marlowe (c. 1597, but published posthumously in the 17th century) – Includes themes of sexual seduction and manipulation.

The Dialogues of Luisa Sigea by Luisa Sigea (c. 1660) – A collection of erotic dialogues, this work was originally written in Latin by a Spanish woman and covers a range of sexual topics.

Erotopolis: The Present State of Bettyland by Charles Cotton (1684) – A humorous work that describes an imaginary land and its sexual practices, it was considered scandalous for its time.

The Gentleman's Academy by 'Philopornos' (1688) – This English text discusses sexual positions and offers advice on sexual matters, written in a pseudo-educational style.

A Treatise of the Pleasures of Conjugal Love by Jean Fernel (c. 1630) – This French work discusses the joys of marital love and was seen as explicit for its time.

The School of Women by Nicolas Chorier (c. 1660) – A French erotic novel that explores sexual relationships and behavior.

Emergence in the 18th Century

The 18th century witnessed a gradual shift in literary sensibilities. As writers began to test the boundaries of both language and societal norms, the emergence of profanity became more pronounced.

John Cleland's *Fanny Hill* (1748)

In 1748, John Cleland penned *Fanny Hill*, a novel that celebrated the pleasures of the flesh and desire. The book's frank and explicit language, coupled with its exploration of sensuality, pushed the boundaries of what was deemed acceptable in literature. Cleland's audacious work ignited passionate debates and faced significant backlash and censorship, yet it served as an early harbinger of literary profanity. You guessed it, the book was a huge hit.

Here are some more in that vein:

The Monk by Matthew Lewis (1796) – This Gothic novel explores themes of sexuality and corruption within the clergy and has been considered scandalous for its time.

The 120 Days of Sodom by Marquis de Sade (Written in 1785, first published in 1904) – Although not published in the 18th century, this infamous work by the Marquis de Sade explores extreme sexual and violent themes.

Dangerous Liaisons by Pierre Choderlos de Laclos (1782) – This epistolary novel delves into the sexual intrigues and seductions of the French aristocracy.

La Religieuse (*The Nun*) by Denis Diderot (Written in the 1760s, first published in 1796) – Although published posthumously, this novel tells the story of a young woman who is forced into the convent against her will and experiences sexual abuse.

Pamela, or Virtue Rewarded by Samuel Richardson (1740) – While not explicit by modern standards, this novel deals with the seduction and attempted seduction of the protagonist Pamela.

The School of Venus by John Cleland (Published in 1680, but widely circulated in the 18th century) – This erotic manual provides advice on sexual techniques and positions.

The Metamorphosis of Lisibetta by Lorenzo Magalotti (1673, but continued to be read in the 18th century) – This libertine novel explores sexual encounters and liaisons.

The Lustful Turk by Anonymous (1788) – This erotic novel features a harem setting and explicit sexual content.

Before moving on it is worth looking into the author John Cleland, who crops up several times as a creator of wanton literature.

John Cleland (1709-1789) was an English novelist best known for his controversial and erotic novel, *Fanny Hill, or Memoirs of a Woman of Pleasure*, which was published in two installments in 1748 and 1749. Born in Kingston upon Thames, Surrey, Cleland came from a somewhat unconventional background. He was the son of William Cleland, a Scottish soldier, and Lucy DuPass, who was of French descent.

Cleland's early life was marked by financial instability, and he entered the British East India Company's service at a young age. His time in India provided him with various experiences, some of which may have influenced the sensual and exotic elements present in his later writing.

In the mid-18th century, Cleland achieved notoriety with the publication of 'Fanny Hill,' an explicit and often humorous novel that explored the sexual adventures of its titular character. The book's vivid descriptions of sexual encounters and its social satire led to its suppression and legal controversy. Cleland himself faced prosecution for obscenity, but he managed to avoid severe punishment.

Despite the controversy surrounding *Fanny Hill*, Cleland continued to write and publish various works, including essays, translations, and memoirs. He spent time in debtor's prison and struggled financially throughout his life. John Cleland's legacy is primarily tied to *Fanny Hill*, which remains a landmark in the history of erotic literature and censorship. His work continues to be studied for its historical and literary significance, reflecting the changing attitudes toward sexuality in the 18th century.

The Victorian Era and Suppression

The Victorian era, characterized by a heightened sense of morality and decorum on the surface, witnessed a concerted effort to suppress explicit content in literature and poetry.

Thomas Hardy's *Jude the Obscure* (1895)

In 1895, Thomas Hardy released *Jude the Obscure*, a novel that dared to confront societal norms with its unvarnished portrayal of sexuality and social issues. The novel broached themes of adultery and sexual desire, making it a prime target for censorship and condemnation. Hardy's boldness in addressing these taboo topics marked a significant turning point in the evolution of profanity within literature. Unlike previous work it was not an instant success, but it is still in print today unlike so many other less scandalous books.

Here is a list of a pick of the 19th Century's scandalous literature:

Madame Bovary by Gustave Flaubert (1857) – This novel explores the life and sexual desires of Emma Bovary, a woman trapped in a loveless marriage, and was seen as morally scandalous in its time.

The Woman in White by Wilkie Collins (1860) – This sensational novel features themes of deception and forbidden love, and it includes a character who escapes an oppressive asylum.

The Awakening by Kate Chopin (1899) – This novel explores female sexuality and independence, as its protagonist, Edna Pontellier, challenges societal norms.

Venus in Furs by Leopold von Sacher-Masoch (1870) – This novella delves into themes of masochism and sexual submission and is known for influencing the concept of 'masochism.'

Là-bas (Down There) by Joris-Karl Huysmans (1891) – This novel contains descriptions of decadent and perverse behavior in the late 19th-century Parisian occult subculture.

The Kreutzer Sonata by Leo Tolstoy (1889) – This novella explores themes of jealousy, sexual frustration and the destructive consequences of an obsessive sexual relationship.

Teleny, or The Reverse of the Medal by Anonymous (Oscar Wilde is often rumored to have been one of the authors) – Published in the 1890s, this homoerotic novel explores a passionate love affair between two men.

Carmilla by J. Sheridan Le Fanu (1872) – A Gothic novella featuring a lesbian vampire, this work was provocative for its time.

The Picture of Dorian Gray by Oscar Wilde (1890) – While not explicitly sexually scandalous, Wilde's exploration of aestheticism, hedonism, and the corruption of the soul through sin made this novel controversial.

The 20th Century and Breaking Boundaries

The 20th century ushered in a seismic shift in literary and poetic expression. Writers cast aside convention and embraced explicit language as a means to convey their narratives with raw intensity.

George Bernard Shaw's *Pygmalion* (1913)

In Act 5 of the play, Eliza Doolittle, one of the main characters, exclaims, 'Walk! Not bloody likely. I am going in a taxi.' This use of language was quite provocative for its time and contributed to the play's controversy and impact. Mrs. Campbell, the actress playing the character, was considered to have risked her career by speaking the line on stage. Bloody was respectable before the mid-1700s, but was heavily taboo from there on after until after the first world war. Dr Johnson considered it a 'horrid word' heavily used by the lower orders but rarely on the lips of the upper crust.

D.H. Lawrence's *Lady Chatterley's Lover* (1928)

D.H. Lawrence's *Lady Chatterley's Lover* stands as a groundbreaking work that delved into themes of love, desire, and class struggle. The novel's explicit language and sexual content were considered scandalous at the time. Its publication and subsequent trials marked a watershed moment in the literary treatment of profanity, sparking heated debates about artistic freedom and censorship.

J.D. Salinger's *The Catcher in the Rye*

In the realm of literary profanity, there exists a pivotal moment marked by the appearance of the word 'fuck' in J.D. Salinger's iconic novel, *The Catcher in the Rye*. Published in 1951, this coming-of-age classic features a narrative brimming with teenage angst and rebellion. The protagonist, Holden Caulfield, uses the word 'fuck' several times throughout the novel, notably when he scrawls it on a school wall. This bold and unapologetic usage of profanity in a mainstream novel during the mid-20th century was groundbreaking and resonated deeply with readers.

Salinger's audacious choice to incorporate such explicit language not only added authenticity to Holden's character but also reflected the changing times and the desire for literature to grapple with the raw realities of youth. This moment in *The Catcher in the Rye* would forever leave its mark on the evolution of profanity in literature, demonstrating its capacity to capture the raw emotions and experiences of a generation. Today no one would bat an eye.

The Contemporary Landscape

In the modern era, profanity and explicit language have become more prevalent and accepted within literature and poetry. Writers no longer bow to societal taboos, and language is wielded as a tool for unfiltered expression.

Bret Easton Ellis's 'American Psycho' (1991)

Bret Easton Ellis's *American Psycho* is a notorious example of contemporary literature that refuses to shy away from explicit language and graphic content. The novel, centered around a psychopathic protagonist, delves into themes of violence, consumerism, and the emptiness of modern life. Its unflinching portrayal of brutality and profanity stirred controversy and ignited discussions about the boundaries of artistic expression.

Poetry's Profane Frontier

Poetry, too, has ventured boldly into the realm of profanity, with poets wielding explicit language to convey their emotions and messages with unrestrained fervor. Yet let us not forget the use of 'fvccant' in the 1400s or Lord Byron whose escapades were infamous as evidence that poets have always been on the edge.

Allen Ginsberg's *Howl* (1956)

Allen Ginsberg's *Howl* stands as a seminal work of Beat poetry that shook the literary establishment with its raw, unvarnished language and exploration of societal issues. The poem delves into themes of drug use, sexuality, and disillusionment, challenging the norms of its time. Ginsberg's fearless use of explicit language became a hallmark of Beat poetry, serving as a catalyst for the counterculture movement.

Outcomes and Reflections

The emergence and progression of profanity within literature and poetry have left an indelible imprint on the literary landscape. While some works faced censorship and controversy, others opened doors for candid discussions about societal taboos and the bounds of artistic freedom.

The legacy of literary profanity is one of artistic courage and unbridled expression. Writers and poets have harnessed explicit language to confront societal norms, challenge conventions, and plumb the depths of the human experience. Through their works, they have pushed the boundaries of language and ignited debates about the role of literature in reflecting and shaping culture.

Conclusion: The Unfinished Story

As we bring our exploration of profanity in literature and poetry to a close, it becomes evident that this journey is far from over. Literature and poetry remain ever-evolving mediums, and writers and poets continue to fearlessly venture into the uncharted territories of explicit language.

In the world of words, where ink dances with imagination, a delicate tension persists between what is deemed acceptable and what is too audacious, between tradition, innovation and obscenity. Profanity in literature and poetry is a testament to the power of language to challenge, provoke and illuminate. It is an ever-unfolding narrative that invites us to grapple with the complexities of human expression and the boundaries of artistic freedom – a narrative that reminds us that the world of words is, indeed, boundless.

Chapter 15:
100 Obsolete Swear Words That Died

There exists a curious phenomenon which is delightfully absurd. It is the phenomenon of words once donning the robes of profanity, only to cast them off and parade through the lexicon as commonplace, everyday citizens. You see, language, like a carnival of linguistic acrobatics, has a way of turning the most scandalous utterances into ordinary expressions.

Consider, for a moment, the word 'bloody.' Once upon a time, this crimson-tinted adjective was regarded with such scandalous disdain that it sent Victorian sensibilities into a flurry. The mere utterance of 'bloody' would make grandmothers clutch their pearls and society matrons swoon in horror. But how times have changed! Today, 'bloody' is as innocuous as a rain-soaked umbrella, a word that punctuates sentences without raising an eyebrow. It is no more shocking than a tea cozy.

And what of 'darn?' In days of yore, this word was a euphemistic shield, protecting innocent ears from the fiery depths of profanity. One might have exclaimed, 'Darn it all!' when vexed by life's capricious whims. Yet, the word itself was but a mere stitch in the fabric of linguistic decorum, a polite alternative to the more colorful expression, 'Damn.' Nowadays, 'darn' and even 'damn' might be considered almost pleasant.

But let us not forget the exuberant exclamations of 'golly' and 'gee.' Once strong language but now regarded as quaint remnants of a bygone era, these words now dance through our conversations if ever as a comical affectation. A mere 'Golly, that's impressive!' or 'Gee, that's surprising!' serves as a testament to their newfound innocence. They have shed their former associations with shock and awe and instead frolic in the fields of everyday playfulness.

And then there's 'crap.' Ah, the word that once stirred feelings of distaste and disapproval. It was the sort of word you might have uttered under your breath when stepping on a piece of wayward Lego in the middle of the night. Yet, today, 'crap' is unlike to earn gasps of scandalized horror.

These examples illustrate a curious truth about language – it is a living, breathing entity that thrives on evolution. The labels we attach to words, whether they be profane or commonplace, are byproducts of collective agreement and societal norms. Words such as 'bloody,' 'darn,' 'golly,' and 'crap' have, over time, undergone a transformation akin to a caterpillar becoming a butterfly. They have shed their taboo cocoons and emerged as beautiful, everyday expressions. What exactly is a 'jerk' or for that matter 'jack' when you don't know jack. Is it the same jack as you find at 'jack in a box?'

To 'jerk' in America means to masturbate, thus a jerk, in English English, is a 'wanker.' So it is surprising that in 1979 a film starring Steve Martin was called *The Jerk*. Would a British film ever be called 'The Wanker.' Perhaps one should be, it would certainly grab attention. So to complete the American swear word malfunction, in the phrase 'you don't know jack,' jack replaces the evergreen or perhaps ever brown swear word 'shit.' So why create a food brand easy to associate as 'shit in a box?' Surely not even a marketing jerk would come up with such an idea!

But what, you might ask, of those words that still reside in the shadowy realm of profanity? Are they forever bound to their scandalous origins? Not necessarily. Language has a way of surprising us. Just as 'bloody' and 'darn' once made their escape from linguistic purgatory, so too might other words find their redemption in the future.

Consider the humble 'fudge.' It's a word often used to sweeten exclamations when a stronger expression might be deemed impolite. Might there come a day when 'fuck' stands proudly alongside 'golly' and 'gee' as a word divested of any of its profane associations? Only time will tell, but it is already far along the process of being defanged.

In the end, the journey of words from profanity to normalcy is a testament to the ever-changing nature of language. It is a reminder that the power of words lies not only in their definitions but in the collective agreement of those who wield them. As we continue to shape and reshape our linguistic landscape, we should keep in mind that even the most scandalous utterances may one day find their place among the everyday expressions that color our conversations. So fear not the evolution of language, for it is a carnival of linguistic wonders, where even the most profane can become, well, quite ordinary.

Here are some of the words once considered scandalous, but now harmless:

Balderdash
Ballyhoo
Ballyrag
Blasted
Blimey
Bloody
Brouhaha
Cheese and rice
Crap
Crikey

Cripes
Dagnabbit
Dang
Darn
Dash it
Dilly-dally
Dingleberry
Donnybrook
Doodad
Doohickey
Durn
Egad
Fandangle
Fandango
Fiddle-dee-dee
Fiddle-faddle
Fiddlesticks
Flibbertigibbet
Flimflam
Flipping
Flummox
Folderol
Fopdoodle
For Pete's sake
Frickin'
Froufrou
Fudge
Gadzooks
Gaggle
Gee
Gibberish
Gizmo
Gobbledygook
Goldarn
Golly
Golly gee
Good grief
Gosh
Gosh darn
Great Scott
Heck

Hell
Higgledy-piggledy
Hobnob
Hocus-pocus
Holy cow
Holy moly
Holy smokes
Hooey
Hootenanny
Hullabaloo
Jeepers
Jeez
Jibber-jabber
Jiminy
Jumpin' Jehoshaphat
Kerfuffle
Land sakes
Lollygag
Malarkey
Mercy
Miscreant
Nincompoop
Ninnyhammer
Nonsense
Poppycock
Ragamuffin
Riffraff
Rigmarole
Sam Hill
Scallywag
Scoundrel
Shenanigans
Shoot
Son of a gun
Sugar
Tally-ho
Tarnation
Thingamajig
Thunderation
Watchacallit
Whatchamacallit

Whatnot
Whippersnapper
Whoopee
Widget
Zounds

The Top Three Swears: No 2

Hold on a minute, this is a good natural break to introduce the second most feared swear word in the English language. The big three were for a long time words that could not be broadcasted, but as time has passed and sensitivities numbed, so they have elbowed their way onto the public stage.

While euphemistic No 2 was number 3, number two is taken by:

Fuck

The etymology of the word 'fuck' is a complex and controversial topic, as it is considered one of the most profane and taboo words in the English language. Its history is shrouded in speculation, and it has evolved over centuries to become the versatile and potent word we know today.

The origins of 'fuck' can be traced back to early Middle English and even earlier languages. To fully understand its history, we must examine its various linguistic predecessors and how it evolved into the word we use today.

Proto-Indo-European Roots

The word 'fuck' can be traced back to its Proto-Indo-European (PIE) roots, which are estimated to date back more than 4,000 years. The PIE root word *pug- or *puḱ-, which means 'to prick,' 'to stab,' or 'to penetrate,' is believed to be the linguistic precursor to 'fuck.' This root word had a sexual connotation in ancient languages and contributed to the development of words related to sexual activity in various Indo-European languages.

Old English and Middle English

The word 'fuck' began to take shape in the English language during the Old English period (circa 5th to 11th century). While it didn't exist in its modern form, the Old English language had several words and phrases related to sexual intercourse and bodily functions. Words like 'fūc' and 'fýc' were used to describe sexual activity and were related to the PIE root *pug-.

During the Middle English period (circa 11th to 15th century), the word 'fuck' began to emerge more explicitly. It was often spelled as 'fuke' or 'fug' and was used to describe sexual intercourse. However, it was still considered a relatively mild term compared to what it would later become.

The Shift to Vulgarity

The word 'fuck' gradually evolved from a relatively innocuous term for sexual intercourse into a highly offensive and taboo word. This shift can be attributed to several factors, including changes in societal attitudes toward sexuality, religion and language.

During the Middle Ages, the Catholic Church exerted significant influence over language and morality in Europe. As a result, words related to sexual activity and anatomy were often considered sinful or vulgar. The Church's influence on language played a role in the increasing taboo status of 'fuck.'

The Renaissance period (14th to 17th century) witnessed a revival of classical learning and the emergence of humanism, which encouraged a more open exploration of human experiences, including sexuality. This period also saw a loosening of linguistic taboos, and words like 'fuck' began to gain more prominence in everyday speech.

Printed Literature and Censorship

The advent of the printing press in the 15th century led to increased dissemination of written material, including books and pamphlets that used the word 'fuck' in various contexts. This further solidified its presence in the English language.

However, as societal norms and censorship efforts evolved, authorities began to suppress the use of explicit language, including 'fuck.' In 1604, the publication of the English translation of the Bible, known as the King James Version, sought to replace explicit terms with euphemisms. This influenced the way sexual terms were used and referred to in English literature.

Modern Usage and Controversy

The word 'fuck' continued to evolve and gain notoriety through the centuries, becoming one of the most potent and controversial words in the English language. It has been used to convey a wide range of emotions, from anger and frustration to pleasure and surprise. Its versatility and intensity have made it a central part of slang and colloquial language.

In the 20th century, 'fuck' became more accepted in popular culture, appearing in movies, music and literature. It was also used as a symbol of rebellion and counterculture movements. Its shock value and power to provoke have made it a subject of debate and legal battles regarding freedom of speech and censorship.

Global Influence

The word 'fuck' is not limited to the English language. It has influenced the vocabularies of many other languages, often adopted as loanwords or integrated into slang. It has a global presence, transcending linguistic and cultural boundaries.

In conclusion, the etymological history of the word 'fuck' is a journey through time and linguistic evolution. From its ancient Indo-European roots to its controversial modern usage, 'fuck' has transformed from a simple word related to sexual intercourse into a powerful and versatile term with profound social, cultural, and linguistic significance. Its journey reflects the complex interplay between language, society and human expression throughout history.□

Chapter 16:
Pop Culture's Obsession with Shock Value

Where every facet of society seems to vie for attention, there exists a sideshow attraction that has consistently captivated audiences and left a lasting imprint – a phenomenon known as 'shock value.' In this chapter, we delve deep into the phenomenon of pop culture, a world where profanity becomes a vibrant and electrifying force, challenging conventions, sparking controversy, driving sales and sometimes even rewriting the rules. Here, we will explore famous examples from both sides of the Atlantic – the United States and the United Kingdom – examining how and why pop culture has harnessed the power of profanity, often using it as a potent tool for various purposes, including attention-seeking, marketing, differentiation, authenticity, ethics and philosophy. This journey will take us through the corridors of media, music, fashion and beyond, unraveling the stories of profanity in pop culture that have shocked, inspired, and defined generations.

The Allure of Attention

In pop culture, where visibility often trumps substance, the magnetic pull of profanity lies in its uncanny ability to seize attention. Whether in headlines, lyrics or public discourse, profanity stands as a neon sign amid the cacophony of modern life, beckoning the curious and daring them to take a closer look.

Marketing and Differentiation

In the world of commerce and branding, where standing out from the crowd is paramount, profanity can be a double-edged sword. While it may alienate some, it can also act as a potent differentiator, setting a brand apart from the sea of competitors.

The French Connection UK (FCUK)

Few examples illustrate this principle better than the fashion brand French Connection UK. In the late 1990s, they unleashed their iconic 'FCUK' logo, a cheeky play on words that deftly balanced on the edge of acceptability. This audacious branding move was both a play on their initials and a tongue-in-cheek allusion to a more explicit phrase. The resulting 'FCUK' logo became an emblem of the brand's irreverent spirit and a statement of nonconformity. It was bold, edgy and, yes, profane. The audacious move not only garnered attention but also etched the brand into the collective memory of consumers worldwide. Profanity, in this context, wasn't just a shock tactic; it was a branding strategy – a deliberate choice to differentiate themselves from the more conservative competition.

The Quest for Authenticity

Pop culture thrives on the pursuit of authenticity – a quality that is often elusive in a world dominated by image crafting and artificiality. Profanity, in its raw and unfiltered form, has frequently been associated with authenticity, making it a sought-after element for artists, musicians, and performers.

Punk Rockers' Rebellious Anthem

The punk rock movement of the 1970s was a rebellion against the polished and manufactured sound of mainstream music. Profanity was woven into the very fabric of punk's ethos – a rallying cry against conformity and a declaration of unvarnished authenticity. Bands like the Sex Pistols and The Clash wielded profanity like a weapon, using it to express their frustrations, dissent and disillusionment with the world. Their profane lyrics and audacious performances were a mirror held up to society, reflecting uncomfortable truths that couldn't be ignored. In the cacophony of profanity, punk rock found its voice, and its message of rebellion and authenticity reverberated with audiences who craved a break from the status quo.

Ethics and Philosophy

The relationship between pop culture and profanity is not confined to the realms of attention-seeking and branding; it extends to deeper ethical and philosophical considerations. It raises questions about freedom of expression, the boundaries of art, and the role of language in shaping our world.

Hip Hop's Lyrical Landscape

In the world of hip hop, profanity is not merely a shock tactic; it is a language of rebellion and a means to confront pressing issues of race, class and inequality. Artists like N.W.A. and Public Enemy have used profanity to deliver powerful social commentary, addressing systemic injustices and drawing attention to the struggles of marginalized communities. Their profane lyrics are a reflection of the raw realities they witness and experience, and they use them to hold a mirror to society's inequities. Hip hop's embrace of profanity is a testament to its commitment to authenticity and its role as a vehicle for unfiltered expression.

The Continuing Saga

The story of pop culture's obsession with shock value, anchored in profanity, is far from over. Profanity continues to be a dynamic force that challenges conventions, prompts discussions, and, at times, disrupts the status quo. In an ever-evolving cultural landscape, where the boundaries of acceptability are in perpetual flux, profanity remains a fascinating and polarizing element.

In the grand theater of pop culture, where every act is a balancing act between artistry and provocation, profanity takes center stage. It is a mirror reflecting society's values, a tool for differentiation and a quest for authenticity. Pop culture's obsession with shock value, intertwined with profanity, reminds us that language is a living, evolving entity – a force that can challenge, provoke, and redefine the boundaries of our cultural landscape. So, dear reader, as you navigate the tumultuous seas of pop culture, remember that beneath the shock and awe lies a deeper story – a narrative of expression, identity and the relentless pursuit of authenticity in a world where the audacious often shines the brightest. The journey continues, and the curtain has yet to fall on this captivating saga of shock, language and culture.

Chapter 17:
The Internet Age: Online Swearing and Trolling

In the vibrant landscape of the internet, where every key press reverberates through the digital cosmos, language undergoes a peculiar transformation. It's a realm where swearing evolves, and new forms of profanity are born, often hiding behind the cloak of acronyms. This chapter ventures deep into the labyrinth of online communication, where profanity takes on novel shapes, where acronyms like 'OMG' and 'WTF' become fixtures of our everyday lexicon. We'll explore the intricate connection between internet trolling and profanity, examine how platform providers such as Facebook, YouTube and X/Twitter grapple with the onslaught of online swearing, and unveil the role of artificial intelligence (AI) in moderating the ever-changing landscape of digital language.

The Digital Lexicon

The internet, an ever-expanding universe of interconnected ideas, has fundamentally altered not only how we communicate but also how we convey shock, surprise, or utter disbelief. In this virtual realm, profanity has undergone a remarkable metamorphosis, birthing a unique digital lexicon.

OMG and WTF: The Birth of Acronyms

During the internet's infancy, profanity and creativity found common ground. Users, seeking to express their astonishment or frustration, crafted acronyms like 'OMG' (Oh My God) and 'WTF' (What The Fuck). These linguistic abbreviations allowed individuals to convey the essence of profanity while avoiding explicit words. It was a clever linguistic sleight of hand – a transformation of the profane into the socially acceptable.

However, the journey was far from over. As online communities flourished, they nurtured their own profane lexicons, giving rise to peculiar concoctions like 'LMFAO' (Laughing My Fucking Ass Off), and 'FML' (Fuck My Life). These digital mutations of language teetered on the precipice of acceptability, crafting a unique form of profanity that was simultaneously shocking and amusing.

Trolling and Profanity

The internet, with its vast expanses of virtual real estate, bred a peculiar breed of mischief-maker – the internet troll. Trolls, often emboldened by the anonymity of the digital realm, reveled in the art of provocation. Profanity became their weapon of choice to incite reactions from unsuspecting targets.

Trolling 101: Profanity as Provocation

Trolls deployed a spectrum of tactics, ranging from mild annoyance to full-blown harassment. Profanity was their trusty ally in all endeavors. Trolls would hurl profane insults, vulgar slurs and explicit language like digital grenades, hoping to elicit outrage, shock or frustration from their victims. It was a game of psychological manipulation, with profanity as the bait and the internet as their battleground.

For example: a troll might infiltrate an online discussion about cute puppies and, with a few well-placed profanities, turn it into a heated, expletive-laden argument.

Another might target a celebrity's social media post, showering it with offensive comments and profane language to provoke a response or attract attention.

Reactions of Platform Providers

The ascension of profanity and trolling presented a formidable challenge for platform providers such as Facebook, YouTube and X/Twitter. As stewards of immense virtual communities, they grappled with the delicate task of balancing free expression with the imperative of maintaining safe and respectful online spaces.

The Battle Against Profanity

In the past platform providers deployed a gamut of measures to combat profanity and trolling. These ranged from content filters that automatically flagged and removed offensive language to reporting systems that enabled users to report abusive behavior. Community guidelines were established to define acceptable conduct. Yet the task remained far from straightforward. Profanity can manifest in countless forms, from cleverly disguised words to euphemisms and coded language. The ever-evolving nature of online communication made it a Herculean challenge to stay one step ahead and many no longer bother in any way, limiting banishment and censorship to hate speech.

AI in the Digital Trenches

To confront the surging tide of online profanity, platform providers will and are enlisting the aid of artificial intelligence (AI). Advanced AI models, like ChatGPT, can be deployed to assist in the formidable task of maintaining civil discourse in virtual communities. Rather than censor or delete, AI makes offensive content undiscoverable and hidden from most viewers while picking out behavior in breach of 'terms of service' that can trigger different levels of response, from post deletion to temporary bans to shadow banning to outright de-platforming.

ChatGPT and similar AI systems harnessed the power of machine learning to recognize patterns and context, enabling them to distinguish between benign uses of profanity (e.g. discussing the history of swear words) and harmful, offensive language intended to harass or demean. While AI offered a valuable tool in the battle against profanity, it was not without its challenges. These models make mistakes, misinterpret context or fail to recognize cunningly veiled messages. Striking the right balance between moderation and free expression remained an ongoing struggle, once again, between what is acceptable speech and behavior and what is not.

The Enigma of Online Profanity

As we contemplate the enigma of online profanity, we find ourselves in a world where words once considered taboo have shape-shifted into acronyms and creative expressions that dance on the edge of acceptability. Internet trolls, armed with profanity, continue to roam the digital landscape, their motivations as elusive as the ever-shifting currents of online discourse. Platform providers wrestle with the unenviable task of maintaining order while respecting free expression.

Profanity remains a formidable force – a reflection of our liberty, capacity for creativity, provocation and linguistic innovation. As we navigate this digital frontier, we are reminded that language is a living entity, constantly evolving and adapting to the contexts in which it thrives. In the realm of pop culture's obsession with shock value, profanity is but one actor in a multifaceted drama, demonstrating that the boundaries of language, like the frontiers of our imagination, are ever-expanding. And so the saga continues to unfold in the infinite corridors of the digital world.

Chapter 18:
Swearing in Politics: From Nixon to Downing St

The Nixon Tapes:
Profanity Behind Closed Doors

One of the most notorious episodes of profanity in American politics occurred behind closed doors in the White House during Richard Nixon's presidency. The Watergate scandal, which eventually led to Nixon's resignation, was accompanied by a trail of secretly recorded conversations in which profanity flowed freely.

In one revealing conversation with his chief of staff, H.R. Haldeman, Nixon famously used expletives to vent his frustrations about the media and his political adversaries. While the exact words were redacted in transcriptions as 'expletives deleted' their impact on public perception was undeniable. Nixon's profanity-laden outbursts revealed a side of the president that was at odds with his carefully cultivated public image.

The Nixon tapes serve as a stark example of how profanity can permeate the highest echelons of power, even when shielded from public view. They raised questions about the authenticity of political personas and the stark contrast between public decorum and private language.

Trump's Unconventional Rhetoric:
A New Era of Profanity

Fast forward to the 21st century, and the political landscape witnessed the rise of Donald Trump, a figure known for his unorthodox communication style and penchant for brash language. Trump's use of profanity, often delivered through X/Twitter and public speeches, marked a departure from the more restrained language traditionally associated with presidential discourse.

One of the most emblematic instances of Trump's profanity occurred during a private meeting in which he reportedly used derogatory language to describe certain nations. The incident, referred to as the 'shithole countries' remark, sparked widespread controversy and condemnation. Critics argued that such language was unbecoming of a sitting president, while supporters viewed it as a refreshing departure from political correctness.

Trump's use of profanity was strategic in many ways. It endeared him to a segment of the population that felt unheard by the political establishment, as his candid and unfiltered style resonated with their frustrations. At the same time, it alienated others who viewed his language as offensive and divisive.

The Global Stage: Swearing in International Politics

Swearing in politics is not limited to the United States. Across the globe, political figures have occasionally let profanity slip into their public statements, often with significant consequences.

In the United Kingdom, for instance, former Prime Minister David Cameron faced scrutiny when he was caught on camera referring to a prominent politician from his own party as a 'twat.' Apparently 'many a twitter makes a twat.' It is hard to disagree with this couplet, in as much as twat, if you wish it, can just mean an obnoxious person rather than a unique organ of the female anatomy. The incident, while relatively mild in comparison to some of the language used in American politics, generated headlines and debate about the appropriateness of such language in political discourse. It also demonstrates how slang words for the same thing can nonetheless carry different weights, twat being on the borderline of acceptable usage, while the use of 'cunt' remains well out of bounds even today.

In Australia, former Prime Minister Julia Gillard delivered a fiery speech in Parliament in which she famously accused the opposition leader of sexism and misogyny. While not profanity in the traditional sense, her pointed language and scathing critique made headlines worldwide. Gillard's speech illustrated how strong language can be employed as a political weapon to address issues of gender and discrimination.

Swearing and the Political Persona

The use of profanity in politics raises intriguing questions about the authenticity of political personas. On one hand, it can be seen as a reflection of unfiltered thoughts and emotions, providing a glimpse into the more human side of political figures. On the other hand, it can be a calculated strategy to connect with certain demographics or to convey frustration.

Politicians who dare to swear walk a fine line, as their language can either endear them to their base or alienate a broader audience. It also underscores the evolving standards of political discourse and the shifting boundaries of what is considered acceptable language for public figures.

In the ever-evolving world of politics, where communication is paramount, swearing remains a potent tool for politicians seeking to communicate their message, express their frustrations, or connect with their constituents. It is a reminder that even in the most formal and structured of arenas, the power of language, both decorous and daring, continues to shape the political landscape.

Chapter 19:
Swear Words in Advertising and Marketing

The Shock Factor:
Provoking Emotions for Profit

Advertising is often a battle for attention in a noisy and crowded marketplace. With consumers bombarded by countless messages daily, marketers need a way to break through the noise and make their brands memorable. Enter profanity, the ultimate attention-grabber.

Profanity has an innate shock factor that seizes the audience's attention. It stirs emotions, whether it be surprise, amusement or even outrage. These emotions create a memorable experience, ensuring that the brand and its message linger in the minds of consumers.

One prime example of profanity's shock value in advertising comes from the United Kingdom. The clothing brand French Connection UK (FCUK) made waves in the early 2000s with its bold and audacious use of the homophonic abbreviation 'FCUK.' The brand's provocative ad campaigns and merchandise, featuring slogans like 'FCUK Fashion' and 'FCUK Advertising,' generated extensive media coverage and discussion. While the use of 'FCUK' was not an overt swear word, it carried the suggestive power of profanity, pushing the boundaries of acceptability in marketing. It not only did not take a crossword genius to work out the anagram, it was hard not to automatically rearrange the letters.

The FCUK phenomenon began in 1997 when the British fashion retailer French Connection sought a way to rebrand itself. Facing financial difficulties and a need for reinvention, the company's marketing team hit upon the idea of using 'FCUK' as an anagram that played on the widely recognized abbreviation 'FC,' often associated with football clubs. The intention was clear: catch the eye, create a buzz and provoke curiosity and focus among consumers.

And create a buzz it did. The 'FCUK' branding became an instant sensation, garnering both praise and criticism. It was seen as audacious, provocative and edgy – all qualities that the brand wanted to convey. The controversial nature of the branding propelled FCUK into the public eye, making it a topic of conversation in various circles.

The Rise and Fall of FCUK

FCUK's branding strategy paid off handsomely, with its revenue and visibility soaring. The provocative ads and merchandise fueled its popularity among young consumers seeking fashion that challenged conventions. FCUK became a symbol of rebelliousness, and its notoriety extended beyond the UK, making it an international phenomenon.

However, as with any marketing strategy that relies on shock value, there came a point of diminishing returns or perhaps diminishing corporate fortitude. Over time, the FCUK branding began to lose its shine. What was once considered daring and edgy became somewhat stale as other brands sought to replicate its formula. Furthermore, some critics argued that the shock value of the 'FCUK' branding overshadowed the quality and substance of the clothing itself, which on reflection seems unlikely as no one would consider their product a luxury brand.

French Connection embarked on a rebranding effort in the mid-2000s. The company gradually phased out the 'FCUK' branding in favor of a more sophisticated and mature image. The decision marked a shift in strategy, as French Connection aimed to distance itself from the controversy and reposition itself in the fashion market.

The rebranding, however, came with its own set of challenges. Removing the iconic 'FCUK' branding meant that French Connection had to find new ways to capture the attention of consumers. It failed. It also had to navigate the transition from a brand known for its provocativeness to one known for its quality and style. If succeed in the first case but failed in the second.

The aftermath of the rebranding was mixed. While French Connection sought to shed its image as a purveyor of provocative fashion, it faced the risk of slipping into relative obscurity. The 'FCUK' branding that had propelled the company into the limelight was gone and with that its fortunes declined.

Lessons from FCUK: The Complex Nature of Profanity in Marketing

The FCUK phenomenon offers valuable insights into the world of profanity in advertising and marketing. It demonstrates the potential of provocative language and imagery to capture attention and create a brand identity that resonates with a specific audience. However, it also illustrates the difficulty of maintaining shock value over time and the challenge of the clash between a strong 'business to consumer' tactic and the desire of the management of corporations for low risk strategies and a quiet life.

The FCUK case highlights the dynamic nature of consumer preferences and the need for brands to align with changing values and sensibilities. What may be considered daring and edgy can fail if corporate management does not have the testicular fortitude to follow it through.

In the end, FCUK serves as a reminder that profanity in advertising and marketing is a double-edged sword. It can catapult a brand to notoriety and success, but it can also lead to downfall. Marketers must walk a tightrope between grabbing their audience without stunning their wider management and stakeholders.

The Art of Subversion: Challenging Norms and Expectations

In the realm of advertising, subversion is a potent tactic, and profanity serves as a vehicle for challenging societal norms and expectations. By deliberately using swear words or profane imagery, marketers can position their brands as rebellious, edgy or counter-cultural. This subversive approach can be particularly appealing to younger, more skeptical audiences.

One of the most iconic examples of subversive advertising through profanity is the marketing campaign of *The Realist* magazine in the 1960s. The publication, known for its satirical and countercultural content, used provocative language and imagery to challenge conventional wisdom and social norms. By embracing profanity, *The Realist* positioned itself as a voice of dissent and garnered a dedicated following among those seeking alternative perspectives.

The Thin Line Between Memorable and Offensive

While profanity in advertising can be a potent tool for capturing attention, it also treads a fine line between being memorable and outright offensive. Marketers must navigate this delicate balance carefully, as crossing into offensive territory can lead to backlash and harm the brand's reputation.

One notable case of profanity backfiring in advertising is the controversy surrounding the Snickers Super Bowl commercial in 2007. The ad featured two mechanics who accidentally kiss while eating a Snickers bar. The punchline of the ad involved one of the mechanics exclaiming, 'I think we just accidentally kissed.' The ad received backlash from LGBTQ+ advocacy groups, deeming it homophobic and offensive. Mars, Incorporated, the parent company of Snickers, pulled the ad and issued an apology, highlighting the potential pitfalls of using humor and innuendo in advertising.

Cultural Sensitivity and Global Impact

Profanity in advertising also faces the challenge of cultural sensitivity and global impact. What may be seen as edgy or humorous in one culture can be deeply offensive in another. Marketers must be attuned to cultural nuances and avoid inadvertently causing offense.

One striking example of cultural sensitivity in advertising is the global presence of Coca-Cola. The multinational beverage company has successfully adapted its advertising campaigns to diverse cultures while maintaining its brand identity. In some regions, humor and light-heartedness are emphasized, while in others, emotional storytelling takes center stage. Coca-Cola's ability to navigate cultural diversity illustrates the importance of tailoring advertising strategies to resonate with specific audiences.

The Enduring Legacy of Provocative Advertising

While profanity in advertising continues to be a subject of debate and controversy, its enduring legacy cannot be denied. It has left an indelible mark on the world of marketing, challenging norms, provoking emotions, and creating memorable brand experiences.

As we reflect on the role of profanity in advertising and marketing, it becomes clear that it is a double-edged sword. When used strategically and thoughtfully, profanity can elevate a brand, captivate audiences and defy conventions. However, when wielded recklessly or insensitively, it can lead to reputational damage and public outcry.

Ultimately, the world of advertising and marketing will continue to grapple with the power and pitfalls of profanity. It remains a tool that demands careful consideration, creativity and an acute understanding of the audience. As the marketing landscape evolves, so too will the strategies and tactics employed, and profanity will continue to be a captivating and contentious element in the ever-changing world of advertising.

Chapter 20:
Linguistic Analysis: Why Swear Words Pack a Punch

The expression of profanity is as diverse as the societies themselves. Swearing, though often deemed taboo, reveals intriguing insights into the intricacies of human communication. As we embark on this linguistic journey, we'll explore how distinct cultures across Europe, Asia, North America, South America, and Africa employ profanity, shedding light on the colorful and sometimes unexpected facets of this linguistic phenomenon.

Europe

Europe is a continent rich in history and languages, each with its unique swearing traditions. In Spain, for example, the term 'joder' is a versatile expletive that can express surprise, frustration or even admiration. Its widespread use highlights the Spanish penchant for passionate and expressive language. Meanwhile, in the Nordic countries like Sweden and Finland, profanity often revolves around bodily functions and is relatively mild compared to some other regions.

Asia

Asia's cultural diversity is reflected in its swearing practices. In Japan, where politeness is highly valued, profanity is relatively subdued. Instead, the Japanese language relies on subtle nuances and context for effective communication. In contrast, Mandarin Chinese has a wealth of colorful idiomatic expressions that incorporate swear words, creating a unique linguistic landscape. India, with its multitude of languages and dialects, boasts a wide array of profanities, each reflecting the cultural diversity of its regions.

North America

The United States and Canada, often sharing similar cultural influences, also exhibit distinct swearing traditions. English profanity is prevalent in both countries, but the choice of words and their intensity can vary significantly across regions. In the U.S., the use of strong expletives is more widespread, while Canadians tend to be more reserved in their swearing. However, both countries share a love for humor and wordplay, often blending profanity with wit in their expressions. In recent times established English profanities have made the journey across the Atlantic and have somehow lost much of their ferocity. Wanker has a beachhead of sorts but is more a word used in humor to send up the English; and the C word, still far beyond the pail in Britain, fetches up in American with the sort of energy reserved for low order swearing like 'arsehole' in the UK.

South America

South America's swearing landscape is as diverse as its geography. In countries like Argentina, the use of profanity is often lighthearted and employed for humorous effect. The term 'boludo,' for example, can be a friendly jest or a playful insult among friends. Brazil, with its Portuguese language, has a unique set of profanities that reflect its vibrant culture and social dynamics.

Africa

Africa's linguistic diversity extends to its swearing practices. In Nigeria, Yoruba swearing often revolves around invoking spirits and ancestors to curse someone. In contrast, South Africa's multilingual society has given rise to a colorful array of profanities, with each language contributing its unique flavor.

As we journey across continents, we encounter the myriad ways in which profanity is woven into the fabric of society. The cultural contexts that shape swearing are as diverse as the languages themselves, highlighting the deep connection between language and identity.

In many cultures, swearing is a reflection of societal norms, values, and power dynamics. It can be a means of expressing frustration, humor, camaraderie or dissent. Swearing can serve as a release valve for pent-up emotions or as a tool for asserting dominance.

For example, in Japan, where hierarchical relationships are crucial, swearing can be a subtle act of rebellion against authority. Japanese salarymen may use profanity to vent their frustrations in a society that places a premium on maintaining a polite façade.

In South American countries like Argentina, swearing is often intertwined with humor and camaraderie. Friends may affectionately insult each other using profanity as a form of endearment, highlighting the close-knit bonds within the culture.

In contrast, some African cultures view swearing as a potent tool for invoking ancestral spirits to protect or curse individuals. This demonstrates the belief in the supernatural and the interconnectedness of language, spirituality, and daily life.

The unique swearing traditions in these regions illustrate the multifaceted nature of human communication. Swearing serves as a reflection of cultural norms and societal dynamics, revealing the complex interplay between language and identity and as an amplifier of emotional punch.

As we explore these diverse swearing practices, it becomes evident that the role of profanity in communication is far from one-dimensional. It is a dynamic and evolving aspect of language that both shapes and is shaped by the societies in which it thrives.

In conclusion, this chapter has taken us on a journey across continents, unveiling the diversity of swearing practices in different societies. Swearing is not just a linguistic curiosity; it is a mirror that reflects the complexities of human communication and identity.

Dr. Alex Aaronson

Chapter 21:
Swearing Across Cultures:
A Comparative Study

Swearing, unique and controversial, transcends cultural boundaries. As we delve into this chapter, we embark on a journey that takes us around the globe, exploring the fascinating world of swearing practices across diverse societies. From Europe to Asia, North America to South America, and even Africa, swearing reveals itself as a linguistic phenomenon deeply influenced by cultural contexts and historical legacies.

Swearing in Europe:
Traditions and Taboos

Our exploration begins in Europe, a continent rich in linguistic diversity and cultural heritage. Here, swearing practices vary greatly from one region to another, reflecting unique traditions and taboos. In countries like Italy and Spain, swearing often revolves around religious motifs, drawing upon the rich Catholic influence that has shaped their societies for centuries. In contrast, Northern European nations such as the Netherlands and Sweden tend to favor more explicit and scatological forms of profanity.

One fascinating example from Europe is found in Italy, where blasphemy is deeply ingrained in the culture. Swearing by invoking the name of the Madonna or other religious figures is not uncommon. The strong connection between religion and profanity highlights how cultural and historical factors can profoundly influence swearing practices.

In Spain, swearing often takes on regional variations, with unique phrases and expressions tied to different parts of the country. In Catalonia, for instance, one might hear someone exclaim 'collons,' which translates to 'testicles' in English but is used as a general exclamation of frustration or surprise. These regional variations showcase the diversity of swearing within European cultures, but also illustrate a biological theme of exclamation across cultures.

Asia: A Mosaic of Language and Tradition

Venturing eastward, we encounter Asia, a vast continent with a plethora of languages and traditions. Here, swearing can take on unique forms, often tied to cultural norms and values. In Japan, for instance, the use of profanity is generally rare, and politeness in language is highly emphasized. However, when it does occur, it often involves derogatory terms related to family or social status, reflecting the importance of hierarchy and respect in Japanese society.

In India, a diverse nation with numerous languages and cultures, swearing varies widely depending on the region. Profanity in Hindi, for example, differs significantly from that in Tamil or Bengali but yet often returns to transcending themes of natural stupidity and sexual organs.

Hindi

Bhosdike (भोसड़ीके): This profanity in Hindi is a derogatory term, often used to insult someone by questioning their intelligence or character. It's literal meaning is 'son of a prostitute.' It is considered highly offensive and vulgar.

Madarchod (मादरचोद): Another strong expletive in Hindi, this term refers to someone as a 'motherfucker.' It is an explicit insult that is likely to provoke a strong reaction.

Chutiya (चुतिया): This word is used to call someone a 'fool' or an 'idiot.' It's a common insult in Hindi and is considered offensive.

Randi (रंडी): In Hindi, this term refers to a prostitute. Using it as an insult is highly offensive, as it not only insults the person but also stigmatizes sex workers.

Lauda (लौड़ा): This word is a colloquial term for the male genitalia. When used as an insult, it's meant to demean someone by questioning their masculinity.

Tamil

Punda (புண்டா): In Tamil, this term is a strong profanity that refers to the female genitalia. Using it as an insult is highly offensive and disrespectful.

Thayoli (தாயோளி): This derogatory term in Tamil is used to insult someone by implying that they are foolish or gullible.

Podai (பொடை): This word is an offensive slang term for the male genitalia. Using it as an insult is considered vulgar.

Koothi (குத்தி): In Tamil, this term is a derogatory reference to a woman's genitalia. Using it as an insult is disrespectful and offensive.

Ammavi (அம்மாவி): This term is used to insult someone by implying that they are acting foolishly or making a mistake.

Bengali

Boka (বোকা): In Bengali, this term is used to call someone a 'fool' or an 'idiot.' It's a common insult and is considered offensive.

Chor (চোর): This word in Bengali means 'thief.' When used as an insult, it accuses someone of being dishonest or untrustworthy.

Shorom (শরম): This term is used to shame someone by implying that they lack shame or decency.

Khanki (খাংকি): In Bengali slang, this word is used to insult someone by questioning their character or morality.

Putki (পুটকি): This term is a vulgar reference to the female genitalia. When used as an insult, it is highly offensive and disrespectful.

The cultural and linguistic diversity of India offers a fascinating glimpse into the intricate relationship between language and swearing and how even with diverse languages many of the ideas driving profanity are shares across humanity.

North America:
From Taboos to Taboos

Our journey then takes us to North America, where the swearing landscape is shaped by a complex history of indigenous cultures, European colonization and immigration. In the United States, swearing practices have evolved over time, often reflecting societal norms and generational shifts. Swear words that were considered taboo in the past may have lost some of their potency in contemporary American society.

For instance, the once highly offensive term 'damn' has become relatively mild in modern usage. However, other words, such as racial slurs, have not only retained their offensive power but have increased in their offensiveness and continue to be deeply controversial. The evolving nature of swearing in the United States demonstrates how language adapts and transforms in response to cultural shifts.

In Canada, a culturally diverse nation, swearing practices can vary significantly between English-speaking regions and French-speaking Quebec. English Canadians may use more Americanized swear words, while Quebecois profanity often includes unique expressions rooted in French language and culture. This linguistic divide reflects the influence of both Anglophone and Francophone traditions. Here are a few unique examples not used in standard French:

Tabarnak (also spelled Tabarnac or Tabarnouche) – A strong profanity derived from the word 'tabernacle.' It's often used to express anger, frustration or emphasis, similar to the English word 'fuck.'

Calice (also spelled Câlice or Calisse) – Another profanity associated with religious items, specifically the chalice. It's used in a similar context to 'tabarnak' and is considered offensive.

Ciboire (also spelled Ciboire or Siboire) – This is yet another profanity involving a religious object, the ciborium. It's used in expressions of anger or frustration.

Crisse (also spelled Crisse or Crissement) – This word is used as a profanity similar to 'damn' or 'damn it' in English. It's not as strong as some of the other Quebecois profanities.

Hostie (also spelled Ostie or Hôstie) – Yet another term derived from religious symbolism, this word refers to the communion host. It can be used as a profanity in expressions of frustration or annoyance.

South America: Expressing Passion and Emotion

Our exploration continues to South America, a continent known for its rich cultural diversity and vibrant traditions. In countries like Argentina and Mexico, swearing often serves as a colorful means of expressing passion and emotion. Swear words may be woven into everyday conversation, and their usage can vary significantly depending on the context.

For example, in Argentina, the term 'carajo,' originally referring to the crow's nest on a ship, has evolved into a versatile exclamation used to convey frustration, excitement, or surprise. It exemplifies how swear words can take on unique meanings and nuances within specific cultural contexts.

In Brazil, a nation celebrated for its Carnival and festive spirit, swearing can be lighthearted and humorous. The Portuguese language offers a plethora of colorful expressions that Brazilians use to convey a wide range of emotions, from amusement to annoyance. Swearing is often embraced as an integral part of Brazilian culture, reflecting the nation's vibrant and expressive character.

Dr. Alex Aaronson

Africa:
A Continent of Languages
and Perspectives

Our final stop on this global tour brings us to the diverse continent of Africa, where a multitude of languages and perspectives intersect. Swearing practices in Africa are as varied as the continent itself, shaped by indigenous traditions, colonial legacies and contemporary influences.

In Nigeria, a country with over 500 languages, swearing can be a complex affair, with different regions favoring distinct profanities. The Yoruba people, for instance, have their own set of swear words that reflect their cultural values and beliefs.

In South Africa, a nation marked by its history of apartheid and diverse linguistic communities, swearing often reflects the complex social dynamics at play. Profanity can be used to express frustration with racial inequality or to challenge the status quo. The linguistic diversity of South Africa gives rise to a rich complex of swearing practices, each offering a unique perspective on the nation's evolving identity.

Conclusion: The Universality
and Diversity of Swearing

As we conclude our journey through the diverse landscapes of swearing practices, we recognize both the universality and diversity of this linguistic phenomenon. Swearing knows no cultural bounds, yet it adapts and evolves in response to the unique contexts and traditions of each society.

Our exploration highlights the intricate relationship between language and culture, revealing how swearing serves as a reflection of societal norms, historical legacies and the ever-shifting dynamics of human communication. As we continue to navigate the world of profanity, we gain a deeper appreciation for swearing's role in communication and expression worldwide.

Chapter 22:
Gender and Swearing: A Sociolinguistic Perspective

The intersection of gender dynamics and swearing provides a complex tangle of complexities. This chapter delves deep into the sociolinguistic aspects of gender and profanity, a journey that unfolds against the backdrop of shifting paradigms in how we choose to view, understand and define gender.

The Unraveling of Traditional Gender Definitions

Once upon a time, gender was often understood within a binary framework – male and female. However, the modern period has witnessed a seismic shift in our perceptions of gender, as definitions have exploded into a kaleidoscope of possibilities. This profound transformation extends its influence far beyond the realm of pronouns and titles; it profoundly impacts the way we engage with language and, yes, swearing.

In examining this transformation, it's crucial to consider how language can both reflect and perpetuate gender stereotypes or, conversely, serve as a tool to explode and reshape them. Here, we encounter a potent interplay between societal norms, language evolution, and the ongoing journey toward gender equality, including within the LGBTQ+ community.

The Language of Stereotypes: Reinforcing or Challenging Norms

Language has a remarkable ability to both reflect and reinforce societal norms. Historically, swearing, like much of language, has been shaped by the prevailing power structures and hierarchies. In this context, gendered profanity has often been used as a means of reinforcing traditional gender roles and reinforcing harmful stereotypes.

For instance, in the UK and the US, derogatory terms targeting women have persisted for centuries, reflecting deeply ingrained patriarchal norms. These terms, while offensive and demeaning, have been employed to assert dominance and reinforce the subservient position historically assigned to women. Examples include slurs that demean women through derogatory descriptions or objectification, or using feminine words about men to imply their weakness.

Challenging the Status Quo: Redefining Gender and Language Within the LGBTQ+ Community

However, the evolving landscape of gender and societal attitudes has also given rise to a powerful counter-narrative. Language, including swearing, has emerged as a battleground for those seeking to challenge the status quo and redefine gender norms, including within the LGBTQ+ community.

In both the UK and the US, LGBTQ+ movements have played a pivotal role in reclaiming language and subverting traditional gendered profanity. Terms that were once used to demean and marginalize individuals based on their gender identity or sexual orientation have been reclaimed and repurposed as symbols of empowerment. LGBTQ+ communities have been at the forefront of reshaping language to be more inclusive and affirming.

Navigating the Nuances: Gender and Swearing in Everyday Life

In the labyrinthine world of swearing, individuals of different genders, sexual orientations and gender identities navigate a nuanced terrain. Their choices of profanity reflect not only personal expression but also societal expectations, peer influences and the evolving discourse around gender, particularly within the LGBTQ+ community.

For instance, the UK has seen a rise in gender-neutral language and swearing within LGBTQ+ spaces. Terms like 'queer' and 'non-binary' have undergone a transformation in contemporary usage. They've become identifiers embraced by individuals who reject traditional gender norms and embrace the fluidity of gender and sexuality.

In the US, similar shifts have occurred, with gender-neutral and affirming language becoming increasingly common within LGBTQ+ communities. The evolution of language reflects an ongoing journey toward inclusivity and recognition of diverse gender identities and sexual orientations.

Conclusion: The Complex Dance of Gender, Sexuality, and Swearing

As we journey through the sociolinguistic landscape of gender, sexuality and swearing, we encounter a complex dance – one that reflects the evolving understanding of gender and sexual diversity within our society and within the LGBTQ+ community. Language, including profanity, both mirrors and shapes our perceptions of gender and sexual identities, offering a window into the profound transformations reshaping our cultural norms.

In this chapter, we've witnessed the power of language to reinforce or challenge stereotypes, and how individuals of different genders, sexual orientations and gender identities navigate the multifaceted world of swearing. The journey towards linguistic inclusivity, gender equality and the redefinition of norms is ongoing, with LGBTQ+ communities playing a central role in this transformation. Language, as always, remains a dynamic force at the heart of this evolving narrative – a force that reflects, challenges and ultimately shapes our understanding of gender, sexuality and swearing, both within and beyond the LGBTQ+ community.

Chapter 23:
The Psychology of Swearing: Catharsis or Harm?

In the curious world of language, where words can evoke a spectrum of emotions, swearing stands as a linguistic anomaly, intriguing psychologists, linguists and curious minds alike. This chapter embarks on a journey through the labyrinthine corridors of the human psyche, exploring the intricate relationship between swearing and the human mind. It is here that we unravel the enigma of whether swearing serves as a cathartic release or possesses the potential to cause harm. As we traverse this terrain, we will encounter famous instances in both the UK and the US, citing specific examples and quotes that shed light on the emotional and cognitive complexities of swearing.

Swearing Across Classes:
A Sociolinguistic Perspective

Before delving into the psychological aspects of swearing, it's imperative to acknowledge that the usage and perception of profanity vary significantly among social classes. Language, including swearing, serves as a distinguishing marker of social identity and class distinctions. The working class, middle class and upper class each have their unique relationship with profanity.

Working Class:
Swearing as a Cultural Norm

In the working-class milieu, swearing often thrives as an integral part of the linguistic landscape. It is not just a tool of communication but a cultural norm, ingrained in daily life. For many, profanity becomes an outlet for expressing frustration, camaraderie or emotional intensity.

'Swearing is just how we talk,' explained Dave, a construction worker with deep roots in the working-class community. 'It's not meant to offend; it's just the way we express ourselves. You hear it on the job site, at the pub, everywhere. It's part of our culture.'

Swearing in the working class serves as a linguistic bridge, connecting individuals through shared colloquial expressions. It is often seen as an authentic and unfiltered form of communication, reflecting raw emotions and genuine interactions.

Middle Class: Straddling the Line Between Politeness and Expression

The middle class occupies a unique position in the sociolinguistic landscape, straddling the line between the working class's colloquialism and the upper class's emphasis on propriety. Swearing in the middle class often finds itself in a delicate balance, influenced by context and company.

'I swear occasionally, but it depends on the setting,' noted Sarah, a marketing executive. 'In professional situations, I avoid it completely. But among friends, especially in informal gatherings, it can be a way to connect and loosen up.'

In the middle class, swearing is often associated with casual and informal interactions. It may be used strategically to convey emphasis or shared experiences without straying too far from social norms of politeness and decorum.

Upper Class: Politeness Prevails

Within the upper echelons of society, where propriety and decorum reign supreme, swearing is a rare and carefully measured linguistic phenomenon. The upper class places a premium on eloquence, restraint, and adhering to established norms of etiquette.

'We were always taught that swearing was a sign of poor breeding,' said Emily, an heiress to an old-money fortune. 'In our circles, one's ability to communicate eloquently and gracefully is valued above all else. Swearing is considered gauche and unnecessary.'

In the upper class, swearing is often viewed as a breach of social etiquette and a departure from the expected standards of linguistic refinement. The emphasis is placed on articulateness and the ability to convey thoughts and emotions without resorting to profanity.

Swearing and the Brain: Short-Term Catharsis or Long-Term Harm?

Swearing's impact on the human brain is a subject of ongoing fascination for researchers. Does it provide a cathartic release, a momentary escape from emotional turmoil, or does it potentially harm our psychological well-being over time?

In the short term, swearing can indeed offer a sense of catharsis. When we encounter a stubbed toe, a frustrating traffic jam or an unexpected mishap, a well-timed expletive can provide an instant release of pent-up emotions. It's as if the verbal outburst acts as a pressure valve, allowing us to vent our frustrations and momentarily alleviate discomfort.

'Swearing can be an immediate emotional outlet,' explained Dr. Linda, a psychologist specializing in emotional regulation. 'It can help individuals express anger, frustration, or pain in the moment. In this sense, it can serve as a coping mechanism for dealing with acute stressors.'

However, the long-term effects of swearing on the brain are a more complex matter. While occasional swearing may offer temporary relief, excessive and habitual use of profanity can potentially desensitize individuals to its emotional impact. Over time, the cathartic effect may diminish, requiring more profanity to achieve the same emotional release.

Furthermore, swearing's impact on interpersonal relationships should not be overlooked. Excessive use of profanity can strain relationships and lead to conflicts, as individuals may perceive it as disrespectful or offensive. In this sense, swearing's short-term relief can come at the cost of long-term harm to social bonds.

Swearing Through the Lens of Freudian Psychology: The Unleashing of the Id

To fully comprehend the psychological intricacies of swearing, we must delve into the world of Sigmund Freud and his pioneering model of the human mind. Freud's tripartite model, consisting of the id, ego and superego, offers a fascinating framework for understanding the motivations behind our use of profanity. As we explore the id-driven nature of swearing, we'll journey through the labyrinthine corridors of the psyche, unravelling the layers of our desires, impulses and the unfiltered release of emotions.

The Freudian Model: Id, Ego, and Superego

Before we embark on our exploration of swearing within the Freudian framework, it's essential to grasp the basic tenets of his model:

The Id: Often referred to as the 'primal' or 'pleasure' principle, the id represents the most primitive part of the psyche. It operates on the basis of immediate gratification, driven by instincts, desires, and impulses. The id disregards societal norms, morality and rationality, pursuing its own pleasure-seeking agenda. The Id is the uncontrollable toddler.

The Ego: Acting as the mediator between the id and the external world, the ego strives to find a balance between fulfilling the id's desires and adhering to societal norms. It operates on the 'reality' principle, employing reason and rationality to make decisions that consider both the id's impulses and the superego's moral standards. The ego is the young reproducing adult.

The Superego: The superego represents the internalization of societal and moral values. It serves as the conscience, enforcing moral standards and ethical behavior. The superego strives for perfection and can induce feelings of guilt and shame when an individual's actions deviate from its standards. It is the adult figure of authority.

Now that we have a foundational understanding of Freud's model, we can explore how swearing fits into this intricate psychological landscape.

In this model the id swears constantly, the ego swears occasionally and only under pressure and the super ego rarely swears and only under the greatest duress when their iron self-control shatters.

Swearing as an Expression of the Id

Swearing, in its rawest form, aligns closely with the workings of the id. It is the id's unfiltered release of emotions, desires and impulses, often bypassing the ego's rationality and the superego's moral constraints. Profanity emerges as a direct expression of our immediate emotional states, driven by the instinctual pursuit of pleasure or the release of tension. Swearing manifests as an expression of a lack of self-control.

Let's delve into specific aspects of swearing through the Freudian lens:

Emotional Catharsis: Swearing can provide an immediate emotional release when confronted with frustrating or distressing situations. Consider the classic example of stubbing a toe – a sudden and intense burst of pain triggers an unpremeditated expletive. This verbal outburst, driven by the id, serves as a cathartic release, offering momentary relief from discomfort.

'Swearing can be a spontaneous emotional release,' explained Dr. Rachel, a psychologist specializing in emotional regulation. 'It's as if the id momentarily takes control, allowing individuals to vent their frustrations and alleviate immediate distress.'

The Pursuit of Pleasure: The id operates on the pleasure principle, relentlessly seeking immediate gratification of desires and impulses. Swearing, in certain contexts, aligns with this principle. When used in moments of joy, excitement or pleasure, profanity can underscore the intensity of the experience.

'In celebratory contexts, swearing can enhance the expression of joy and enthusiasm,' noted Dr. Daniel, a researcher in linguistics and emotions. 'It's as if the id celebrates the pleasure of the moment through linguistic intensity.'

Spontaneity and Impulsivity: The id is characterized by spontaneity and impulsivity. Swearing often emerges spontaneously, without prior planning or forethought. In moments of surprise, shock, or even delight, profanity can burst forth as an immediate and unmediated response.

'Swearing's impulsivity aligns with the id's tendency to act on instinct,' explained Dr. Olivia, a psychoanalyst. 'It's a glimpse into the unfiltered psyche, where emotions and instincts take precedence over societal norms.'

Emotional Authenticity: Swearing, in its unadulterated form, can be an authentic expression of an individual's emotional state. When we swear, we reveal a facet of our inner selves that may remain concealed in everyday interactions. It's as if the id momentarily sheds the layers of social conditioning, allowing us to express our genuine untamed emotions.

The Id and Swearing: A Complex Relationship

While swearing's alignment with the id is evident, it's crucial to recognize that the id's pursuit of immediate gratification can sometimes lead to conflicts within the psyche. The id may clash with the ego's rationality, prompting inner turmoil as we navigate the tension between our unfiltered impulses and societal norms.

In moments of emotional intensity, the id's dominance may result in the unbridled use of profanity, even when such language contravenes social decorum. This interplay between the id and the ego reflects the complexity of swearing's psychological impact.

In our exploration of swearing through the Freudian lens, we've illuminated its close association with the id – the primal, pleasure-seeking aspect of the human psyche. Swearing emerges as an unfiltered release of emotions, desires and impulses, often bypassing the ego's rationality and the superego's moral constraints. As we continue our journey through the psychology of swearing, we'll uncover further layers of its impact on the human mind, offering a comprehensive understanding of this linguistic phenomenon.

Swearing in Jungian Psychology: The Shadow Self and Authentic Expression

In the realm of psychology, the name Carl Gustav Jung looms large, and rightfully so. Jungian psychology offers a unique lens through which we can explore the profound intricacies of swearing. At the heart of Jung's theories lies the concept of the 'shadow self,' a fascinating facet of human consciousness that sheds light on why we swear, what it means, and how it affects us on a deeper level.

To delve into Jung's world of psychology is to embark on a journey into the recesses of the human psyche, where the shadow self resides. This section will not only explore the shadow self and its connection to swearing but also the broader implications of Jung's insights for our understanding of profanity as an authentic form of expression.

The Shadow Self: Unveiling Hidden Depths

Carl Jung, a Swiss psychiatrist and psychoanalyst, introduced the concept of the shadow self as a fundamental component of his analytical psychology. The shadow self represents those aspects of our personality that are hidden, often repressed, and typically considered unacceptable by societal norms. It encompasses our unacknowledged desires, instincts, emotions and traits that we conceal from ourselves and others.

The shadow self is not inherently negative; rather, it embodies the totality of our being, including those aspects we have deemed unworthy, embarrassing or morally objectionable. These facets often include anger, lust, envy, greed and yes, profanity. Swearing, in this context, can be seen as an expression of the shadow self, a means of giving voice to emotions and desires that may remain concealed in everyday interactions.

In this model, swearing can be a way of revealing the parts of ourselves that we hide, it allows us to express emotions that society might deem inappropriate or taboo unless marked as such. In doing so, swearing can be a form of kind of punctuation to meaning.

Jung believed that acknowledging and integrating the shadow self is crucial for personal growth and psychological wholeness. To deny or suppress these hidden aspects can lead to inner conflict, projection onto others and a lack of self-awareness. Swearing, when used authentically and consciously, can serve as a channel for recognizing and embracing these concealed dimensions of our psyche.

Authentic Expression: Swearing as Emotional Honesty

One of the key tenets of Jungian psychology is the idea of individuation – the process of becoming one's true self by integrating all aspects of one's personality, including the shadow self. In the context of swearing, this process involves acknowledging profanity as a facet of human expression rather than rejecting it as mere vulgarity.

'Swearing, when used authentically, can be a form of emotional honesty,' explained Dr. Mark, a Jungian therapist. 'It's a departure from the polished personas we present to the world. In our daily lives, we often wear masks, concealing our true feelings and desires. Swearing can strip away those masks, revealing our unvarnished selves.'

Jungian psychology encourages individuals to confront and accept their inner contradictions and complexities. Swearing, in its raw and unfiltered form, can be a vehicle for such confrontation. It provides a space where our hidden emotions, frustrations and desires can be expressed without the veneer of societal expectations.

The Shadow in Action: Swearing as Shadow Work

Jungian shadow work is a therapeutic process that involves exploring and integrating the shadow self into one's consciousness. It is a journey of self-discovery and self-acceptance, often guided by a trained therapist. Swearing, surprisingly, can be an inadvertent catalyst for this process.

Consider a scenario where a normally composed and polite individual suddenly lets loose a torrent of profanity in a fit of anger. In that moment, the shadow self emerges, unburdened by societal norms and politeness. This eruption of profanity can be seen as a glimpse into the hidden recesses of the individual's psyche.

The use of profanity in such moments can be an invitation to explore the shadow. The shadow seizes the opportunity to express itself when we are momentarily overwhelmed. Recognizing and reflecting on these outbursts can lead to greater self-awareness.

Swearing can act as a mirror, reflecting our inner conflicts, frustrations and desires. Jungian shadow work involves engaging with these reflections, recognizing them as part of our authentic selves and integrating them into our conscious identity.

Jung and the Collective Unconscious: Swearing as Cultural Expression

Jung's theories extend beyond the individual psyche into the realm of the collective unconscious – a shared reservoir of universal experiences, symbols and archetypes that connect humanity across cultures and time. Within this collective unconscious, language, including profanity, takes on a cultural significance that transcends individual expression.

'Swearing can also be viewed as a cultural expression of the collective shadow,' said Dr. Alec, a Jungian scholar. 'Profanity often reflects the hidden tensions, conflicts, and taboos within a society. It's a linguistic mirror of our collective psyche, highlighting the aspects we struggle to confront as a culture.'

In this context, profanity serves as a linguistic artifact that reflects the cultural values, norms, and repressed emotions of a given society. Swearing can provide valuable insights into the collective psyche, shedding light on societal taboos and shared emotional undercurrents.

Conclusion: Swearing and the Shadow Self

As we navigate the intricate terrain of Jungian psychology and swearing, we unearth a profound connection between profanity and the shadow self. Swearing, when examined through the lens of the shadow, becomes a gateway to authenticity, self-discovery, and cultural exploration.

Jung's insights invite us to view swearing not as a mere linguistic quirk but as a window into the depths of our individual and collective psyches. Swearing reveals the concealed facets of our personalities, the unspoken tensions of our culture, and the raw emotions we often suppress in our quest for social conformity.

In embracing and understanding swearing as an expression of the shadow self, we embark on a journey of self-acceptance and self-awareness. We confront the contradictions and complexities within us, leading to a deeper understanding of our true selves and the multifaceted nature of the human experience.

Dr. Alex Aaronson

The Language of the Mind: Profanity as an Expression of Emotion: A Post Post-Modern Take

Exploring the intricate relationship between swearing and psychology offers valuable insights into the human experience. Profanity, as we investigate it, becomes a fascinating gateway to understanding the interplay of emotion, culture and individualism within our society.

At its core, swearing serves as a unique means of emotional expression. It provides an unfiltered channel for individuals to convey their deepest emotions, particularly during moments of heightened intensity. When we swear, we tap into a reservoir of genuine, unvarnished feelings that conventional language may struggle to capture. Profanity can be seen as a way to authentically communicate our emotions, offering a release valve for pent-up frustrations and passions.

In the Stoic tradition, which encourages emotional self-control and rationality, the act of swearing can be viewed as a reflection of our inner turmoil and a potential obstacle to achieving inner tranquility. The Stoics advocate for mastering one's emotions and cultivating wisdom, virtues and self-discipline. From this perspective, profanity may be seen as a symptom of unchecked passions rather than a means of genuine expression.

Beyond individual psychology, swearing is intricately linked to the broader context of culture and societal norms. Profanity doesn't exist in a vacuum; it mirrors the taboos and boundaries that define a culture. It delineates the lines between socially acceptable discourse and what's considered transgressive. In this way, swearing becomes a linguistic marker that reflects the evolving values, ethics and dynamics of power within a society. It's a barometer of cultural evolution, highlighting the ever-changing landscape of language and expression.

Moreover, swearing underscores the importance of individual autonomy and freedom of expression. The choice of language, including the use of profanity, becomes a vital aspect of personal sovereignty. It represents an individual's right to express themselves authentically, free from undue societal constraints. A society that respects this freedom in language values personal autonomy and the diversity of human expression.

In conclusion, swearing emerges as a complex and multifaceted linguistic phenomenon that connects our innermost emotions, mirrors evolving societal norms, and celebrates personal autonomy in language. While it may conflict with Stoic ideals of emotional self-mastery, it still offers insights into the intricate interplay of human emotions. This exploration invites us to consider not just the words we use but also the profound psychological, cultural, and philosophical dimensions that underpin our linguistic expressions. Swearing, in all its intricacies, serves as a rich platform through which we can delve into the depths of human psychology and the ever-evolving landscape of language and society.

Conclusion: Profanity's Psychological Landscape

As we navigate the intricate terrain of swearing's psychology, we encounter a rich channel of emotional release, social norms and the depths of the human psyche. Swearing is a multifaceted linguistic phenomenon that can provide momentary catharsis, reflect cultural and class distinctions, and offer a glimpse into the complexities of the human mind.

Whether we view swearing through Freud's id-driven lens or Jung's exploration of the shadow self, it remains an integral part of our linguistic repertoire. It is a tool for emotional expression, a reflection of cultural values and a mirror into the depths of our individual and collective psyches.

In the ever-evolving landscape of language and psychology, swearing continues to captivate researchers, linguists and individuals alike. Its complexities invite further exploration, shedding light on the intricate interplay between language, emotions and the human experience.

Chapter 24:
Swearing in the Workplace:
A Delicate Balance

The workplace is a space where individuals from diverse backgrounds and experiences come together to collaborate, communicate and achieve common goals. Within this context, language plays a crucial role in fostering effective communication, maintaining a respectful environment and defining professional culture.

However, the workplace is not a monolithic entity. It encompasses a vast spectrum of professions, each with its own unique culture, norms and expectations regarding language use. Swearing in the professional sphere, therefore, presents a delicate balance that varies widely depending on the industry and the specific job roles within it.

Everyday Swearing:
Where Expletives Are Part of the Job

In certain professions, swearing is not just commonplace; it is an integral part of the job. Industries such as construction, manufacturing and the military are often characterized by environments where expletives are everyday occurrences. These vocations demand clear and direct communication, often in high-stress situations, where swearing can serve as a form of shorthand, conveying urgency, frustration or danger.

One of the most iconic examples of this phenomenon is the construction industry, where colorful language is as much a part of the toolkit as a hammer or a wrench. Construction workers are known for their creative and colorful vocabulary, using expletives to convey crucial information, relieve tension and maintain safety protocols.

In these professions, swearing is not taken personally; it is a tool of the trade, a means of efficient communication in high-pressure situations. It is an unspoken agreement among colleagues that expletives are a functional aspect of their professional language.

The Forbidden Realm: Where Swearing Is Taboo

Conversely, there are industries where swearing is not only rare but vehemently discouraged or even forbidden. The realm of finance, law and academia, for instance, upholds a strict code of professional conduct that places a premium on decorum and precision in language.

In the world of finance, where millions of dollars can hinge on a single decision, maintaining a composed and dignified demeanor is paramount. Swearing is viewed as unprofessional and detrimental to the image of financial institutions.

Navigating the Consequences: The Fine Line Between Professionalism and Inappropriate Language

Swearing in the workplace, whether accepted or discouraged, carries consequences that can shape careers and reputations. It is a fine line to tread, and individuals must exercise discernment and restraint when choosing their words.

Outbursts serve as cautionary tales, illustrating the potential damage that profanity can inflict on one's professional standing. In the world of academia, where intellectual discourse thrives, the use of offensive language can disrupt the pursuit of knowledge and respectful exchange of ideas.

Benefits of Swearing in the Workplace: A Paradoxical Perspective

While the pitfalls of swearing in the workplace are evident, there is a paradoxical perspective that suggests potential benefits in certain situations. Swearing, when used judiciously, can convey urgency, release tension and even foster camaraderie among colleagues.

In high-pressure professions like healthcare, where life-or-death decisions are made daily, the occasional expletive may serve as a pressure valve, allowing healthcare workers to cope with the immense stress they face.

Swearing, in these instances, is not about offense or disrespect but rather a pragmatic tool for navigating the challenges of the profession.

Managing Swearing in the Modern Workplace

In the modern workplace, the dynamics of swearing are evolving alongside broader societal shifts. Many organizations now recognize the need for clear guidelines on language use, emphasizing professionalism and respect while acknowledging that occasional lapses may occur.

Organizations often implement diversity and inclusion training to address language-related issues and promote respectful communication. This approach seeks to strike a balance between fostering a comfortable and inclusive environment while upholding professional standards.

The Future of Swearing in the Workplace

As we gaze into the future, the role of swearing in the workplace remains in flux. It is influenced by changing attitudes toward language, evolving workplace cultures and shifting societal norms.

The workplace is a microcosm of society, reflecting its complexities, contradictions and transformations. Swearing, whether as a means of expression or an exception to decorum, will continue to be a subject of discussion, debate and adaptation within the professional sphere.

As individuals and organizations grapple with the intricacies of swearing, they must navigate the fine line between effective communication and maintaining a respectful and inclusive workplace culture. The balance between professional expression and inappropriate language will undoubtedly remain a defining feature of the modern workplace, offering both challenges and opportunities for those who navigate its ever-shifting landscape.

Chapter 25:
The Legal Side: Obscenity Laws and Freedom of Speech

When considering swear words and their place in society, one cannot escape the intricate dance between the legal realm and the realm of language. This chapter embarks on a journey through the legal dimensions of swearing, delving into the complexities of obscenity laws, freedom of speech and the delicate balance that exists between safeguarding individual liberties and upholding societal standards. To navigate this terrain, we'll explore some famous cases in the UK and the US, examining their outcomes, their aftermath and the laws that shape this intricate landscape.

Obscenity Laws: Drawing the Line

Obscenity laws, designed to regulate and restrict the use of offensive language and content, have been a source of debate and contention for centuries. These laws are the legal foundation upon which societies attempt to delineate the boundaries of acceptable language and expression.

In the United Kingdom, the Obscene Publications Act of 1959 was a significant milestone in the country's approach to obscenity. The act made it an offense to publish material that had the potential to 'deprave and corrupt' those who came into contact with it. It marked a pivotal moment in the ongoing battle to strike a balance between the freedom to express oneself and the need to protect the moral sensibilities of society.

Across the Atlantic in the United States, obscenity laws have similarly played a crucial role in shaping the legal landscape surrounding swear words and offensive content. The landmark case of Miller v. California in 1973 established a three-pronged test to determine obscenity, emphasizing the importance of local community standards in defining what is obscene.

Dr. Alex Aaronson

Freedom of Speech: A Fundamental Right

Freedom of speech, enshrined in various forms in both the UK and the US, is a foundational principle that underpins democratic societies. It grants individuals the right to express their thoughts, ideas and opinions without fear of government censorship or punishment.

In the United States, the First Amendment to the Constitution explicitly protects the freedom of speech. It has led to a robust tradition of free expression and has influenced the way the country approaches the regulation of obscenity and profanity. Landmark cases such as Cohen v. California (1971) have defended the right to use profane language as a form of political protest, reaffirming the importance of this constitutional right.

In the United Kingdom, freedom of speech is not enshrined in a single constitutional document but is protected through a combination of common law and statutes. Despite not having a written constitution, the UK has historically upheld the importance of free expression. However, the boundaries of this freedom are continually tested in a society grappling with evolving norms and expectations.

The Complex Dance of Regulation

Regulating profanity in a legal context is akin to a delicate dance, where lawmakers and courts must navigate the treacherous waters of protecting individual liberties while also safeguarding societal standards. This dance has given rise to numerous famous cases that have shaped the legal landscape of swearing.

One such case in the United States is the 1978 Supreme Court decision in FCC v. Pacifica Foundation, often referred to as the 'Seven Dirty Words' case. Comedian George Carlin's 'Filthy Words' monologue, broadcast on a New York radio station, sparked outrage and led to a legal battle over the Federal Communications Commission's authority to regulate indecent content on the airwaves. The Supreme Court ruled in favor of the FCC, establishing that the government had the right to restrict certain offensive language during times when children were likely to be in the audience.

In the United Kingdom, the 1960 trial of Penguin Books for publishing D.H. Lawrence's novel *Lady Chatterley's Lover* marked a watershed moment. The case revolved around whether the novel's explicit sexual content and profanity constituted obscenity. The trial, which included the famous question, 'Is it a book that you would even wish your wife or your servants to read?' ultimately ended in acquittal. It was a significant victory for freedom of expression and a pivotal moment in the ongoing debate over obscenity laws in the UK.

The Ongoing Debate

As we navigate the legal dimensions of swearing, we find ourselves in an ongoing debate that spans continents and generations. The tension between preserving individual liberties and upholding societal standards remains at the heart of this discourse.

In the United States, cases like Snyder v. Phelps (2011) have tested the limits of free speech, as the Supreme Court ruled in favor of the Westboro Baptist Church's right to use offensive language during protests at military funerals. The decision upheld the principle that even deeply offensive speech is protected under the First Amendment.

In the United Kingdom, recent controversies surrounding online hate speech and the potential harm it can cause have reignited discussions about the balance between free expression and the need to protect individuals from harm. New laws and regulations are being proposed to address these challenges, further highlighting the ongoing evolution of legal frameworks in response to changing social norms.

Conclusion: A Delicate Balance

In the intricate lexicon of swear words and their legal regulation, we find a delicate balance between preserving the fundamental right to freedom of speech and upholding societal standards of decency. The legal dimensions of swearing are ever-evolving, shaped by landmark cases, shifting norms, and the ongoing struggle to strike the right balance.

As we reflect on the legal landscape of swearing, we are reminded that the tension between individual liberties and societal norms is an enduring one. It is a tension that reflects the complexity of human expression and the evolving nature of language itself. Swear words, at the intersection of language and law, continue to be a subject of fascination and debate, serving as a mirror to our ever-changing society and its values.

The Top Three Swears: No 1

The ultimate bad word. I'm sure you know which of all profanities is the worst of all. So here it is, without further ado, the history of the number 1 swear word.

Cunt

The word 'cunt' is undoubtedly one of the most controversial and offensive words in the English language. Its etymological history is a complex and contentious one, marked by centuries of evolution, taboo, and social stigmatization. Despite its shocking nature today, delving into the word's origins can provide valuable insights into the development of language and the cultural shifts that have shaped it.

The earliest recorded use of the word 'cunt' dates back to Middle English, during the late 13th century. In this period, it was spelled as 'cunte' and bore a less offensive connotation than it does today. Back then, 'cunt' was a common term for female genitalia, and it was used without the extreme vulgarity it carries now. It had a straightforward, descriptive function in the language, similar to other anatomical terms.

The origin of 'cunt' in Middle English can be traced back to various European languages. It is believed to have descended from the Old English word 'cunte,' which also meant female genitalia. Additionally, the word has ties to the Old Norse term 'kunta' and the Middle Dutch word 'kunte,' both of which had similar meanings.

The usage of 'cunt' in the Middle Ages was far from the shock value it holds today. It appeared in medical texts, literature and even street names. For instance, there are records of streets named 'Gropecunt Lane' in medieval England, reflecting the more open and less taboo use of the word during that time. 'Gropecunt' was the equivalent phrase to the modern 'red light district' and like those modern places were often the street names of the busiest areas of town. As 'Cunte' became ruder so the place names became censored, for example bowdlerized to Grape Lane.

As the English language continued to evolve, so did the connotations and acceptability of various words, including 'cunt.' The word underwent a significant shift during the Renaissance period in the 16th and 17th centuries. As the church's influence on language and morality waned, there was a revival of classical Greek and Latin texts. This revival led to the reintroduction of Latin words and a growing awareness of their meanings. In Latin, the word 'cunnus' also referred to the female genitalia. This linguistic reawakening, combined with the influence of Latin, contributed to the word 'cunt' becoming more associated with vulgarity and obscenity.

The taboo surrounding 'cunt' escalated in the 18th and 19th centuries. During this period, society became increasingly prudish and conservative. Words that were once considered acceptable in public discourse were now deemed obscene and offensive. The word 'cunt' became a prime target for censorship and social ostracism. This shift in attitude led to a situation where the word was used less openly and was considered highly offensive, especially when directed at individuals.

The Victorian era, with its strict moral values and rigid social norms, played a significant role in cementing the word 'cunt' as a deeply offensive and unacceptable term. It became associated with vulgarity and indecency, and was generally considered unfit for polite society.

Despite the word's taboo status, it never entirely disappeared from the English language. It continued to be used in underground and subversive contexts, often as a form of rebellion against societal norms and censorship. In some cases, it was employed to challenge prevailing views on sexuality and gender roles.

The 20th century witnessed a significant cultural revolution, and with it came changes in language and attitudes toward words like 'cunt.' The sexual liberation movement of the 1960s and 1970s challenged traditional views on sex and language, advocating for more open discussions about sexuality. The feminist movement also played a crucial role in reclaiming and redefining the word 'cunt.' Some feminists sought to destigmatize it, viewing it as a symbol of female empowerment rather than an insult.

By the late 20th century, 'cunt' began to appear more frequently in popular culture, literature and comedy, albeit often used for shock value or comedic effect. It was also reclaimed by some individuals and groups as a way to subvert the word's derogatory history and assert their own empowerment.

In recent years, there has been an ongoing debate about the word 'cunt.' While some argue that it should remain stigmatized due to its historical and current use as a misogynistic insult, others advocate for its continued reclamation and use as a way to challenge societal norms and language taboos.

In conclusion, the word 'cunt' has a long and complex etymological history that reflects broader shifts in language and culture. From its innocuous beginnings as a simple anatomical term in Middle English, it evolved into a deeply offensive and taboo word during the Victorian era. However, in more recent times, it has seen a resurgence in usage, with some seeking to reclaim and redefine it. The history of 'cunt' serves as a testament to the ever-changing nature of language and its deep connections to societal norms and values.

Chapter 26: Censorship vs. Freedom: A Contemporary Debate

The enduring debate between censorship and freedom of expression takes center stage in this chapter. It examines how contemporary society grapples with the tension between regulating language and safeguarding individual liberties. By exploring recent developments and controversies, it sheds light on the complex, ongoing discussions that shape the future of speech and censorship.

In a world where words are both our shield and our sword, where the utterance of a single syllable can evoke laughter, outrage or even camaraderie, the debate over the boundaries of speech rages on. It is a debate that encompasses all corners of society, from the halls of power to the street corners where people exchange their daily gossip. The tension between censorship and freedom of expression, like the push and pull of opposing tides, has been a constant presence in the human narrative.

As we navigate the choppy waters of contemporary society, it is essential to consider the multifaceted attitudes towards swearing that various social groups hold. These attitudes are as diverse as the words themselves, reflecting the human experience. To understand the complexities of this debate, we must delve into the perspectives of different social groups and explore how they shape and are shaped by their views on swearing.

The Puritans: Guardians of Virtue

In the annals of history, the Puritans stand as staunch defenders of moral righteousness. For them, the use of profanity was not only a breach of etiquette but a transgression against the divine order. They saw themselves as guardians of virtue, tasked with upholding a strict code of conduct. The words they considered profane were not just offensive; they were an affront to their deeply held religious beliefs.

One of the most famous figures of the Puritan era, Jonathan Edwards, sermonized with fervor against profanity. In his famous sermon, 'Sinners in the Hands of an Angry God,' he thundered, 'The profane swearer, the drunkard, the adulterer – all stand before God as guilty of death.' For the Puritans, swearing was a sin that threatened the very fabric of their society.

The Bohemians: Defying Convention

Contrast this with the Bohemians, who reveled in defying convention and embracing the unconventional. To them, swearing was a form of rebellion against the oppressive norms of their time. Bohemian circles, often populated by artists, writers and free spirits, saw profanity as a means of challenging authority and expressing raw, unfiltered emotion.

Oscar Wilde, the iconic wit of the late 19th century, once quipped, 'I can resist everything except temptation.' Wilde's sharp tongue and provocative statements challenged the Victorian moral order, making him a symbol of the Bohemian spirit. His use of language, both eloquent and irreverent, was a testament to his defiance of societal norms.

The Pragmatists: Balancing Act

Amidst the ideological clashes between the Puritans and the Bohemians, the pragmatists sought a middle ground. They recognized the power of language but also understood the need for decorum in public discourse. Pragmatists believed in freedom of expression but advocated for responsible communication that considered the impact of words on society.

Theodore Roosevelt, the 26th President of the United States, embodied this pragmatic approach. He famously stated, 'Speak softly and carry a big stick.' Roosevelt understood the importance of measured speech in diplomacy and governance. While he could be forceful when necessary, he recognized that profanity had its time and place.

The Rebels: Pushing Boundaries

In the ever-evolving landscape of language, rebels continue to push the boundaries of what is considered acceptable. They see profanity as a tool for dismantling oppressive systems and challenging deeply ingrained prejudices. Rebels argue that, by exposing the ugliness of certain words, they can strip them of their power.

Comedian George Carlin was a master of this approach. In his iconic routine, 'Seven Dirty Words,' Carlin dissected and deconstructed profanity with wit and insight. He questioned the arbitrary nature of taboos, challenging society to reevaluate its language norms. Carlin's irreverence made him a hero to those who saw profanity as a means of confronting societal hypocrisies.

The Prudes: Upholding Decorum

On the opposite end of the spectrum, the prudes remain steadfast in their commitment to upholding decorum and maintaining the dignity of language. They argue that profanity corrodes the social fabric and erodes civility. To them, swearing is a sign of moral decay and a slippery slope towards societal breakdown.

Queen Victoria, the epitome of Victorian decorum, famously said, 'We are not amused.' Her reign was marked by strict standards of etiquette and a rejection of vulgarity. She believed that the use of coarse language was beneath the dignity of her court and her empire.

The Future of Speech and Censorship

As we stand at the crossroads of the 21st century, the debate over swearing in society rages on, with each social group championing its perspective. The enduring tension between censorship and freedom of expression is not likely to dissipate anytime soon. Instead, it continues to evolve in response to changing social norms, technological advancements, and shifting cultural landscapes.

The rise of the internet, with its unprecedented access to information and communication, has amplified this debate. Social media platforms, once hailed as bastions of free expression, now grapple with the challenge of moderating content that often blurs the line between legitimate discourse and offensive language.

In this digital age, public figures, celebrities and influencers are scrutinized for their use of language like never before. One ill-considered tweet or offhand comment can spark outrage, leading to a cascade of consequences. The power of words to shape public opinion and influence societal attitudes has never been more apparent.

The Complexity of Moderation

The complexity of moderation on online platforms has given rise to a new set of challenges. What constitutes hate speech, and where does the line between free expression and incitement to violence lie? These questions have led to heated debates and calls for greater transparency in content moderation.

Figures like Mark Zuckerberg, CEO of Facebook, have found themselves at the center of this debate. Zuckerberg has stated, 'We're committed to preventing abuse on our platforms.' However, defining and addressing abuse in a way that satisfies all stakeholders remains a daunting task.

The Battle for Control

The battle for control over language and its limits rages on in legislatures and courtrooms worldwide. Laws against hate speech, incitement and defamation are continually tested in the context of evolving digital communication. In some cases, governments seek to expand their authority to regulate online speech, raising concerns about potential overreach and threats to free expression.

Justice Robert H. Jackson, who served on the United States Supreme Court argued, 'The First Amendment is not a suicide pact.' Jackson emphasizes that free speech must be balanced with the broader interests of society, including protecting vulnerable individuals from harm. Striking this balance is an ongoing challenge for lawmakers and the legal system.

The Role of Education and Media Literacy

Education and media literacy play pivotal roles in shaping attitudes towards swearing and censorship. As society becomes increasingly interconnected, individuals must learn to navigate the digital landscape responsibly. Media literacy programs aim to equip people with the critical thinking skills necessary to assess the veracity and impact of online content.

The words we choose to use and the way we interpret language are influenced by our upbringing, education, and exposure to different cultures and perspectives. In an era where information flows freely and often unfiltered, the ability to discern credible sources from misinformation becomes paramount.

The Future Unfolds

In conclusion, the debate over swearing, censorship, and freedom of expression is a dynamic and evolving conversation. It reflects the intricate interplay of cultural, social, technological, and legal forces. Different social groups bring their unique perspectives to the table, shaping the contours of this ongoing dialogue.

The future of speech and censorship remains uncertain, as new challenges and opportunities emerge. As language continues to adapt and transform, so too will our understanding of what constitutes profanity and the boundaries of free expression. In this ever-changing landscape, one thing remains clear: the power of words to inspire, provoke, and connect us will endure, no matter where the debate takes us.

Chapter 27:
The Future of Swear Words and Language

The future of swear words and their role within our linguistic landscape is a subject ripe for contemplation. As we near the conclusion of our journey through the labyrinthine history of profanity, it is only fitting to cast our gaze forward, peering into the uncertain depths of what lies ahead.

The Enduring Power of Profanity

Swear words, for all their audacious irreverence, have endured the relentless march of time. They've weathered the tides of cultural change, the ebb and flow of societal norms and the ceaseless evolution of language itself. They stand as linguistic titans, stubbornly refusing to fade into obscurity.

Why, you might wonder, do these words persist, despite the ever-present efforts to censor and sanitize language? The answer, it seems, lies in their primal appeal. Profanity, in all its blunt and unapologetic glory, taps into something fundamental within us. It serves as a linguistic release valve, a cathartic expression of frustration, anger or exasperation. These words, like a pressure relief valve on a boiler, allow us to vent our emotions in a controlled manner, preventing the buildup of internal linguistic steam.

While society may wax and wane in its acceptance of profanity, the human need to utter a well-placed swear word remains unwavering. It's an age-old tradition, a linguistic refuge that transcends cultures and generations, linking us to our ancestors who, too, reveled in the art of colorful expression.

The Evolving Role of Profanity

As we gaze into the crystal ball of linguistics, one thing becomes abundantly clear — the role of profanity in society is far from static. It is a shape-shifting entity, forever adapting to the changing currents of human interaction and communication.

In the past, swear words were often wielded as weapons, brandished to insult, demean or offend. They were the linguistic arsenal of the aggressor, used to inflict emotional wounds and provoke outrage. But as society has evolved, so too has the function of profanity.

Today, we find that swear words often serve as a form of social currency – a way to bond, to empathize, or to convey camaraderie. They can be terms of endearment among friends or a shared expression of frustration among colleagues. Swear words, in some instances, have transformed into linguistic tools of solidarity, forging connections and understanding in a world that sometimes struggles to find common ground.

The Ongoing Debates and Linguistic Evolution

As we navigate the uncharted waters of the future, we must acknowledge that the trajectory of profanity is not without its controversies and debates. The battle between those who champion freedom of expression and those who advocate for censorship rages on. Questions of appropriateness, offensiveness and societal impact continue to spark fervent discussions in boardrooms, classrooms, and living rooms alike.

Language, being a living entity, will inevitably continue to evolve. New words will emerge, and existing ones will take on new meanings. Some words that were once considered profane may lose their sting, while others may ascend to the throne of linguistic taboo. The future of swear words is a realm of uncertainty, where only time will reveal the linguistic treasures and pitfalls that await.

The Swear Words of Tomorrow: An Imaginary Expedition

In our musings about the future, let us indulge in a whimsical journey – a playful exercise in linguistic speculation. Just as the swear words of today were once innocuous terms that took a dark turn, what harmless words might become the profanities of tomorrow?

Imagine a world where 'flibbertigibbet' is muttered in hushed tones, its utterance met with gasps of shock and disapproval. Perhaps 'ballyhoo' becomes the ultimate expletive, capable of sending shockwaves through polite society.

'Gobbledygook' might take on a sinister connotation, its use reserved for the most scandalous of situations.

In this fanciful future, our linguistic landscape would be populated with innocuous words-turned-taboo, each carrying the weight of societal judgment. Just as our ancestors could never have foreseen the transformation of once-innocent words into profanities, so too might we find ourselves bewildered by the linguistic flip-flops of generations to come.

The Uncharted Horizons of Profanity

As we conclude our journey through the history of swear words and language, we are left with a sense of wonder and curiosity about what lies ahead. The enduring power of profanity, its evolving role in society, and the debates that shape its trajectory are but a few facets of this intricate linguistic gem.

Language, like the ever-expansive universe, is a realm of boundless possibilities. Swear words, those linguistic mavericks, will continue to play their part, evolving, challenging and provoking in equal measure. And so, as we bid adieu to this exploration of the profane, we step into the uncharted horizons of language, where the future of swearing awaits, like a tantalizing riddle yet to be unraveled in the ongoing narrative of human expression.

The Evolutionary Tide of Language

The canvas of language, as vast and unpredictable as the cosmos, knows no bounds in its continuous evolution. Just as the constellations shift over millennia, so too does our linguistic firmament. The words we hold dear, the ones we fling with fiery fervor, and the utterances that stir our souls – they all partake in the grand dance of linguistic transformation.

To peer into the future of swearing and language is to cast ourselves adrift on the boundless sea of linguistic possibility. As society changes, so do our linguistic norms, our taboos, and the very words we employ to convey our thoughts and emotions. The boundaries we establish today may dissolve into insignificance tomorrow.

The Paradox of Freedom and Censorship

In this ever-changing linguistic landscape, we are confronted with the paradox of freedom and censorship – a balancing act that society must perform delicately. Freedom of expression is a cherished cornerstone of democratic societies, a pillar upon which the edifice of open discourse stands. Yet, in the pursuit of civility and respect, societies must also grapple with the need for restraint and sensitivity.

The debates surrounding the use of profanity and its potential impact on individuals and communities will persist, echoing through the corridors of academia, lawmaking chambers and internet forums. The question of where to draw the line, of what is permissible and what is not, will remain at the forefront of public discourse.

The Linguistic Alchemy of the Future

In our playful musings about the future of swearing, we encounter a tantalizing prospect – the prospect of linguistic alchemy. Innocuous words, once the embodiment of harmlessness, may transform into linguistic grenades, capable of detonating shock and scandal. It is a notion that tickles the imagination, a reminder that language is a living entity, forever shape-shifting.

Picture a world where 'flibbertigibbet' is uttered with caution, a world where 'ballyhoo' is met with disapproving glares, and 'gobbledygook' carries the weight of scandal. In such a world, language itself becomes a playground of linguistic absurdity, a realm where the unlikeliest of words reign supreme.

Yet, let us not forget that the journey of language is one of constant adaptation and evolution. Just as words transition from innocence to infamy, so too do they metamorphose in response to the changing tides of human expression. What may be taboo today may become mundane tomorrow, and what is unspeakable now may become a source of amusement or curiosity in the linguistic playground of the future.

Of Human Expression

As we navigate the uncertain terrain of the future, one thing remains abundantly clear: language, with all its quirks and complexities, is a reflection of the human experience.

In the grand mosaic of human expression, profanity serves as a reminder of our capacity for both restraint and release, for eloquence and expletive. It reflects the ever-shifting boundaries of what is deemed acceptable and unacceptable, challenging us to question and reevaluate our linguistic norms.

As we bid farewell to our exploration of the profane, we embark on a new chapter – one filled with linguistic surprises, evolving taboos and uncharted horizons. The future of swear words and language beckons, a tantalizing riddle that will continue to unravel in the ongoing narrative of human expression. In the end, it is a journey that we, as explorers of language, are fortunate to undertake – a journey that promises to reveal the ceaseless dynamism of the words we hold dear and the ever-evolving nature of human communication.

At the root a profanity is only what people agree is a profanity. A profanity is agreed upon and then used accordingly for its purpose. Douglas Adams, the late author of *A Hitchhikers Guide to the Galaxy* declared 'Belgium' was the worse swearword in the universe, and if agreed to be so, it can become as such however the denizens of Brussels might complain.

Certainly, language is constantly evolving, and words that were once innocent may take on new meanings or connotations over time. Here is a list of 100 existing words, along with their current meanings and explanations of why they have the linguistic potential to become considered profane:

Bumble – Currently means to move clumsily or in a confused manner. Potential for use as a mild insult due to its whimsical sound.

Chatter – To talk rapidly or incessantly. The word's association with excessive speech might lead to playful uses.

Chomp – To bite or chew with a noisy, vigorous manner. Its sound might be associated with aggressive eating.

Chuckle – A quiet, amused laugh. Its association with humor might lead to playful uses.

Clamor – A loud, confused noise. The chaotic nature of the word might suggest tumult.

Clatter – A loud, rattling noise. The word's sound might be used to describe cacophonous events.

Clutter – A collection of disorganized items. The chaotic nature of the word might suggest messiness.

Creak – To make a high-pitched, squeaking noise. The word's sound might evoke images of old, worn objects.

Cringe – To recoil or flinch in anticipation of something unpleasant. Its sound could evoke discomfort.

Cuddle – To hold close for warmth or affection. Its association with intimacy might lead to euphemistic uses.

Dawdle – To waste time or move slowly. The sound of the word could be humorous in certain contexts.

Doodle – To scribble or draw aimlessly. Its association with absentmindedness might lead to playful interpretations.

Fiddle – To play casually on a musical instrument. Its association with 'fiddling around' might lead to connotations of idleness.

Fizzle – To make a hissing or sputtering sound. Its onomatopoeic nature might suggest failure or disappointment.

Flap – To move up and down or back and forth with a waving motion. Its sound could suggest agitation.

Flicker – To shine with a wavering, unsteady light. The word's sound could suggest instability.

Flounder – Means to struggle or stagger clumsily. Its sound could be associated with awkwardness.

Flutter – To move or flap quickly and lightly. The word's sound might suggest excitement or nervousness.

Fumble – To handle clumsily or ineffectively. Its association with mistakes could make it mildly insulting.

Gabble – To talk rapidly and unintelligibly. Its sound may suggest hurried or chaotic speech.

Gamble – To play games of chance for money. Its association with risk-taking might lead to euphemistic uses.

Giggle – A light, playful laugh. The word's sound could be used to describe moments of amusement.

Glide – To move smoothly and gracefully. The word's sound could be associated with elegance.

Gnash – To grind or strike one's teeth together. The word's association with frustration might lead to playful interpretations.

Gnaw – To chew on something persistently. The word's association with tenacity might lead to playful interpretations.

Gobble – To eat quickly and greedily. The word's association with voracious eating might lead to euphemistic uses.

Grumble – To complain or express dissatisfaction. Its association with discontent might lead to mild insults.

Grunt – A low, guttural sound. The word's sound could be used to describe exertion or effort.

Gurgle – To make a bubbling or gurgling sound. The word's onomatopoeic nature might evoke bodily functions.

Gush – To flow forth suddenly and rapidly. The word's sound could be used to describe emotional outbursts.

Hiccup – A sudden, involuntary contraction of the diaphragm. The word's sound might suggest unexpected interruptions.

Hiss – A sharp, sibilant sound. The word's onomatopoeic nature might suggest disapproval.

Hobble – To walk unsteadily. The word's sound might evoke images of limping or difficulty moving.

Jiggle – To move quickly and jerkily. Its playful sound might suggest frivolity.

Jumble – A confused mixture or mess. The chaotic nature of the word could suggest disorganization.

Linger – To stay in a place longer than necessary. Its sound could suggest reluctance or indecision.

Lounge – To sit or lie in a relaxed, lazy manner. Its connotation of idleness might lead to playful interpretations.

Lurch – To make a sudden, uncontrolled movement. The word's sound might suggest unpredictability.

Mingle – To mix or blend. The playful sound might make it a euphemism for more intimate actions.

Muddle – A state of confusion or disorder. The chaotic nature of the word might suggest disarray.

Mumble – To speak in a low or indistinct manner. Its sound could be associated with unclear communication.

Munch – To eat something with a steady, audible chewing. Its sound might be associated with voracious eating or could be used euphemistically for more explicit expressions.

Murmur – A soft, indistinct sound. The word's sound could be used euphemistically for more explicit expressions.

Mutter – To speak quietly and incoherently. Its association with unclear speech might lead to mild insults.

Ponder – To think deeply or consider carefully. Its association with contemplation might lead to playful interpretations.

Pout – To push out one's lips in a sulky or disappointed manner. Its sound might suggest childishness.

Puddle – A small pool of liquid. Its association with water might lead to playful interpretations.

Scribble – To write or draw hastily and carelessly. The word's association with messiness might lead to playful interpretations.

Scuffle – A brief, disorderly fight. The word's sound might lend itself to playful insults.

Shiver – To tremble or shake involuntarily. The word's sound could evoke images of cold or fear.

Shuffle – To move with dragging or scraping sounds. Its sound might be associated with clumsiness.

Sizzle – To make a hissing or crackling sound. Its onomatopoeic nature might suggest excitement or intensity.

Skim – To move lightly and quickly over a surface. The word's sound could evoke images of superficiality.

Skulk – To move stealthily or with a guilty conscience. The word's connotation might lend itself to covert activities.

Slump – To sit, lean, or fall heavily in a relaxed or careless manner. Its sound could be associated with laziness.

Slurp – To make a loud, sloppy noise while drinking or eating. Its onomatopoeic nature might suggest messiness.

Snicker – Presently means to give a half-suppressed laugh. Its similarity to 'snigger' might lead to misinterpretation.

Snore – To breathe noisily during sleep. Its sound could be associated with sleepiness or laziness.

Snuggle – To settle or move into a warm, comfortable position. Its association with intimacy might lead to euphemistic uses.

Sputter – To make explosive or sizzling noises. The word's sound might be used to describe emotional outbursts.

Squabble – A noisy argument, often about trivial matters. Could be used to describe heated disagreements.

Squawk – A loud, harsh cry or sound. Its sound could be associated with annoyance or protest.

Squeak – A high-pitched, sharp cry or noise. The word's sound might be used to describe surprise or alarm.

Squirm – To twist and turn in a wriggling motion. The word's sound could suggest discomfort or restlessness.

Swirl – To move in a twisting or circular motion. The word's sound might evoke images of whirlpools.

Tinkle – To make a high, tinkling sound. The word's onomatopoeic nature might suggest delicacy.

Tumble – To fall suddenly and helplessly. The word's connotation might lead to associations with accidents.

Twiddle – To turn or move something repeatedly in a casual or idle way. Its sound could be associated with triviality or an action of self love.

Twitch – To make a sudden, involuntary movement. Its sound could be associated with nervousness.

Waddle – To walk with short, shuffling steps. Its playful sound could be used humorously.

Whimper – To cry softly or with plaintive sounds. The word's sound could evoke images of vulnerability.

Whine – To complain or express discontent in a high-pitched, irritating manner. Its sound could suggest annoyance.

Whisper – To speak in a soft, hushed tone. The word's connotation might suggest secrecy or intimacy.

Whittle – To carve or cut small pieces from wood. The word's association with craftsmanship might lead to playful uses.

Wiggle – To move with small, quick movements. The playful nature of the word might suggest silliness.

Wobble – To move unsteadily from side to side. The word's sound might evoke images of instability.

Wriggle – To twist and turn in a sinuous or wavy motion. The word's sound might suggest playfulness.

These words, while currently innocent, possess linguistic potential due to their sounds, associations or connotations. As language continues to evolve, some of these words may take on new meanings or connotations, potentially leading to their use as profanities or playful euphemisms in the future. Language, like life itself, is in a perpetual state of flux, where words are both the brushstrokes and the canvas of our ever-changing human experience.

I'm sure you can do better and why not, as certainly some loving son will.

About the Author

Dr. Alex Aaronson is a trailblazing figure in the realm of postmodern anthropology, where he seamlessly intertwines the study of linguistic patterns with the intricate tapestry of Bronze Age burial practices. With a fervent passion for unraveling the mysteries of human culture and communication, Dr. Aaronson stands at the forefront of interdisciplinary research, bridging the gaps between anthropology, linguistics and archaeology. Armed with a keen intellect and insatiable curiosity, Dr. Aaronson delves into the nuances of language, dissecting its evolution and significance within diverse cultural contexts. His lectures captivate audiences as he navigates the complex terrain of linguistic theory, weaving together insights from structuralism, post-structuralism, and beyond.

However, it is in his exploration of Bronze Age burial practices that Dr. Aaronson truly shines. With meticulous attention to detail, he excavates burial sites, piecing together the fragments of ancient rituals and customs. Through his groundbreaking research, he sheds light on the beliefs and social structures of bygone civilizations, offering a glimpse into the rich warp and weave of human history.

As an educator, Dr. Aaronson inspires the next generation of scholars, instilling in them a deep appreciation for the complexities of human culture and language. His interdisciplinary approach challenges conventional thinking, encouraging students to think critically and explore new avenues of inquiry.

Beyond academia, Dr. Aaronson is a prolific author, with numerous publications in prestigious journals and academic presses. His work has earned him widespread acclaim within the academic community, solidifying his reputation as a visionary thinker and scholar.

Dr. Alex Aaronson's contributions to postmodern anthropology are immeasurable, as he continues to push the boundaries of knowledge and understanding in his quest to unravel the intricacies of human culture and communication.

www.ingramcontent.com/pod-product-compliance
Lightning Source LLC
Chambersburg PA
CBHW061644250726
48659CB00004B/1368